ಌಇ

The Accidental Mayor

ಊಬಝ

CBEO

The Accidental Mayor

by

TOMILEA ALLISON AND JAMES ALLISON

CBEO

The Accidental Mayor

This book may be purchased from Amazon.com
and wherever books are sold.

☙❧

Cover and book design by Merridee LaMantia

Belmantia Publishing Services
BelmantiaPublishing@gmail.com

We dedicate this story

*to Bloomington, Indiana,
and all of her children—
especially Devon and Leigh.*

Authors' note: Unless indicated otherwise,
the voice is that of Tomilea Allison.

ACKNOWLEDGMENTS

IT IS SIMPLY NOT POSSIBLE to list everyone who helped us with this book, but here are some who did. For recollections and advice, Devon Allison, Rosemary Miller, Tim Mueller, Steve Sharp, Martha Wainscott, Glenda Murray, and Charlotte Doyle. For early encouragement, two anonymous readers. For encouragement and corrections, Jan Ellis. For their skill in book production the artists of Belmantia Publishing Services, Janet Cheatham Bell (words) and Merridee LaMantia (book & cover design). For comfort and entertainment, the backyard fauna often seen through our dining room window: deer, skunk, possum, squirrel; raccoon, rabbit, robin; starling, jay, nuthatch; flicker, chickadee, cardinal, crow; junco, sparrow, catbird; the titmouse and the wren, the mourning dove and the downy woodpecker. Cooper's hawk. Ocho the Russian Blue. Thanks to them, and more. Any flaws, of course, are ours.

CONTENTS

1. Accidental Mayor..1

2. Early Days 2

3. The Campaign Trail, Miles 1-3 11

4. The Campaign Trail, Mile 4 15

5. Starting Out..19

6. Denver Smith..29

7. The Campaign Trail, Mile 6 44

8. PCBs and I 53

9. The Campaign Trail, Miles 7 and 8............................62

10. Pleasantries...75

11. The Campaign Trail, Miles 9 and 10..........................87

12. Downtown...98

13. Arts and Craft... 107

14. Parks and Recreation 123

15. Social Needs 137

16. The Showers Project 142

17. Planning and Zoning 155

18. Public Works.. 190

19. Facilitative Leadership... 194

Notes 211

Index 221

Vitae... 247

CHAPTER 1

Accidental Mayor

Frank McCloskey, in his eleventh year as Mayor of Bloomington, decided to run for Congress. He had a firm grip on the mayor's office, but Congress was a greased pole. Bloomington had become a liberal Democrat's town, the steady exception in a county, state, and Congressional district that mostly went Republican. In 1982 his opponent was Republican Joel Deckard, heavily favored for a third consecutive term in the 8th District. Few expected McCloskey to win. He would probably be back next year for a fourth term as mayor.

The campaign seemed to run true to form. Congressman Deckard started with a big lead, and appeared likely to hold it throughout. But one night in southern Indiana, three weeks before the election, two events turned everything around. First, an accident: Deckard drove his car into a tree. Second, not so accidentally, he refused to take a blood test and was charged with driving under the influence of alcohol.

Suddenly the challenger surged. The incumbent's comfortable lead melted away. Come election night, the 8th District delivered a big upset: McCloskey 52%, Deckard 48%. Frank went to Congress, Joel went out, and I became mayor of Bloomington.

What? Who was this woman, anyhow, and how did she get to be mayor all of a sudden?

Many saw it that way, and rightly so, but it was not so sudden to others. To tell the whole story, I have to go back to the beginning.

CHAPTER 2

Early Days

I was born at home when that was not so odd, in 1934. The place was Madera, California, a small farm town in the San Joaquin Valley, right on Highway 99. My mother was a farm girl, my father an electrician. She named me Tomilea Joyce. The last name, Radosevich, came from my Croatian immigrant grandfather. "Tomilea" was inspired by two maternal ancestors, Tom and Leah. (It is strange, but not unique, as I learned when in an internet search I was astonished to find another woman called "Tomilea Allison.") When very young I disliked the only normal part of my name, and settled on "Tomi" as my lifelong preference.

In nearby Kerman my maternal grandparents farmed Thompson seedless grapes, the kind you find in a box of Sunmaid Raisins. I remember "The Farm" as our hedge against the hardships of the Great Depression: If things went really bad we could always go there to live. We never had to go, but it was good to know The Farm was there.

I grew up with a brother, Greg, two years older than I, and three male cousins about our age. We were always inventing games together, and I usually directed. I would come up with the ideas and get the others to come along. When Grandfather Radosevich gave us treat money, he kept the boys from fighting by having me carry it.

Outside, in the dirt, our game to build the Burma Road was a romantic favorite, thanks to World War II (WW II) news. Inside the garage, big cardboard boxes became police cars or airplanes. "Calling all cars, that is all; roger wilco, over and out." We were big on radio communications. I collected matchbook covers discarded on the shoulder of the great highway. I hung out near my grandfather's motel, the Dixie Auto Court, hoping to collect the colorful airplane card from any customer who had just bought a package of Wings cigarettes.

Decades later, as I directed a family car trip, my 6-year-old granddaughter looked up and blurted out a daring question: "Grandma, what makes YOU so bossy?" The rest of us laughed, but none could answer her question. I have always been a bit bossy.

During WW II we moved around the state a lot, from one military base to another, as my father's skills as a civilian electrician were much in demand. Finally we settled back in Madera, where I progressed from grammar through high school. We lived on a street with few trees. I vowed that when I grew up I would live in a place with plenty of trees.

I've had an abiding impulse from way back to help anyone against a bully. I had a lot of practice, thanks to a bunch of aunts, uncles and cousins who enjoyed teasing others. I felt sorry for my grandfather, a staid farmer who took a daily afternoon nap with his shoes and socks off. As he slept, my mischievous female cousin painted his toenails with red nail polish. When he awoke they gave him the shock of his life. To deepen his mortification, he thought the nail polish was permanent.

Then came a day when I was old enough to retaliate. That same cousin had played a mean trick on me and my brother when we were so young we could only cry. With our bathing suits under our regular clothes, we walked to a distant creek for a swim. Ready to go home, we found that our cousin had tied our clothes in knots too tight for us to unknot. She had also knotted our laces too tight to get our shoes on. It was a typical summer day in the

San Joaquin Valley, with blazing fields and roads that we had to endure as we trotted home barefoot in our bathing suits.

Many years later she visited again. As she prepared for a heavy date, I offered to draw a bath for her. Into the hot bath water I emptied a bottle of the strongest perfume I could find, Tabu. When I emerged I apologized for the strong odor: I said I had broken a bottle in the bathroom. The unsuspecting cousin took her bath, the perfume permeated every pore, and she smelled like Tabu for days.

A similar motive might explain my notorious high school essay. My civics class required an essay on current events at a time when the California Loyalty Oath was in the news. At the height of a red scare, California had adopted a law that required every state employee to sign an oath of political loyalty to the government. This requirement would apply, for example, to every professor, file clerk and janitor employed by the University of California at Berkeley. The oath had been big news, but I was not deeply aware of the passions it had released, or its significance in world politics, the Cold War, national or internal security.

I did some research, decided what I thought, and wrote my essay. The teacher asked me to give an oral report to the class. I said the oath looked like bullying, and condemned it. When the teacher asked if anyone in the class agreed with my unpatriotic position, I had an instant introduction to the perils of an unpopular political position. Exactly one classmate agreed with me, and none of my friends. It was probably fortunate that he happened to be the star center on the basketball team.

In the days that followed, my speech teacher quietly took me aside. She said, in secret, that she and several other young teachers were proud of me for the position I had taken. This was all very strange and unsettling, because I had taken my position with no sense that it required any special bravery.

Many years later, at a class reunion, I saw the star center again and reminded him of the incident, with gratitude. He had no recollection of the matter.

I had a Presbyterian baptism and accepted the Christian social gospel then as I do now. My mother saw to it that both of her children attended Occidental College, a school with Presbyterian roots. Oxy provided my cultural awakening. My interest in social welfare and how societies worked led me to study sociology. When the Dean of Women said that I needed an activity, I chose the Young Democrats and worked for Adlai Stevenson. I learned about music and the arts, silent movies, cool jazz, Odetta, Maria Tallchief, Jose Greco, Olvera Street and Ensenada. Two classmates became famous, a concert pianist and an opera set designer. Two others were Hollywood children, the son of a famous producer and the son of an actor, well known but not quite famous. Jack Kemp soon followed, and many years later, Barack Obama.

After graduation I returned to Fresno, where we then lived, totally unprepared for a job in public welfare. Not content to hand out checks, I wanted to solve problems. I took postgraduate courses in criminology and social work at Fresno State University. I interned at the Juvenile Division of the Fresno County Probation Office, where I was soon hired as a Deputy Probation Officer, my first full-time job. In high school I had worked in a drug store as a part time clerk and soda jerk. In Los Angeles I had waitressed part time at a Van de Kamp restaurant.

In Fresno I met my future husband. Jim had just returned from U.S. Army service in Germany. A graduate of the University of California at Berkeley, he worked for a year as a Deputy Probation Officer before he went on to Claremont Graduate School. We married and lived in Claremont and Upland for a while, where I became a Deputy Probation Officer for San Bernardino County. We then moved to Ann Arbor, where our two daughters, Devon and Leigh, were born. While Jim studied experimental psychology I read Dr. Spock, *Mother Goose, Winnie the Pooh,*

Rachel Carson, Doris Lessing, Jane Jacobs and I. F. Stone. Jim received his Ph.D. from the University of Michigan in 1963, and we moved to Bloomington that summer.

BLOOMINGTON

Indiana settlers, struck by the flowers and foliage in bloom on its prospective site, named the town Bloomington. Or, maybe the name came from one of those settlers, Mr. William Bloom. Take your pick, or invent your own tale. Where the name came from, no one really knows.

I found volunteer work in Bloomington at the Christian Center, where I met Reverend Marvin Jones. Most of his energy went toward helping the poor take charge of their lives. We founded the Community Development Conference, and encouraged low-income residents of the Pigeon Hill-Crestmont neighborhood to run for public office. Soon we began to protest the Vietnam war.

This work taught me how to run precinct-level political campaigns. In every congressional race our people worked the precincts for antiwar candidates. When my husband's colleague, Jim Dinsmoor, ran a peace campaign in a congressional primary in 1966, I helped organize the campaign. In a presidential primary I managed Senator Eugene McCarthy's campaign in Monroe County.

When the Vietnam war ended we turned our attention to local politics and formed Citizens for Good Government, a slating organization. My daughter, Devon, could tell you how I cajoled her and her sister, Leigh, to spend many an afternoon with me in some dreary room amid long tables and hard folding chairs, stuffing envelopes for the good of humanity and the promise of milkshakes at the end of the day. (Down on the square, Southern Sporting Goods had a tiny soda fountain that made fabulous milkshakes. You sat on a high stool with a full glass, and anticipated the big remainder in your gleaming metal canister.)

My fifteen years in the trenches with like-minded activists had won the trust of many willing workers. One of them was City Councilman Jeff Richardson, with whom I had collaborated on antiwar campaigns when he was Indiana University's (I.U.) student body vice president. It was Jeff who nominated me to fill a vacancy on City Council, my first public office. Five years later, when Frank McCloskey left the mayor's office for Congress, it fell to the Democratic precinct committee members to choose a replacement mayor. Many of them agreed to support me because they knew my work as an organizer. That is how it all began.

But it could never have happened without the Goo Goos.

THE GATHERING OF THE GOO GOOS

In the 1960s local government had a horse-and-buggy aura that reformers found irresistible. These good government types, derided in the east as "Goo Goos" in every smoke-filled room of rough and tumble politics, lived in and around the university community. In terms of the political spectrum they were liberal Democratic outsiders, looking in at the conservative Republicans who seemed firmly and forever in charge.

We saw the Republican style soon after we moved to Bloomington. One evening we took our two young daughters to a public meeting of the city council. If we had any particular reason for attending that meeting, neither of us can recall it. The chamber was empty except for us, a few officials, the mayor and the councilmen, who beamed at the children and gave us a friendly greeting. They went on with their business, but the discussion suddenly halted. They looked at one another, and adjourned briefly to a private room, apparently to continue their discussion in secrecy. When they returned the councilmen conducted a unanimous vote with no further ado. That's how things were done.

The pattern was common enough—a liberal university in a conservative surround—and so might have been the resulting tensions, but for three great things that drove and shaped our actions: civil rights, the war on poverty and the war in Vietnam.

Many of my generation were galvanized into citizen action by the civil rights movement and the example of Martin Luther King, Jr. In a related development, President Lyndon Johnson's war on poverty led me and many friends to make new social ties throughout the community. Together we formed Community Development Conference, which aimed to empower the un-empowered through social integration and political organization. But we were soon diverted by Vietnam and its sudden claim on most of our time and energy. We turned our efforts toward educating ourselves and the public about the war. As public opinion slowly came around, the war and the protests began to subside and we returned our attention to the empowerment of citizens through local politics.

There was no grand beginning, no clap of thunder: We simply needed to figure out who deserved our votes. A local election would suddenly come up, but we would have no idea who the candidates were, what they believed or what they thought important. Party affiliation was no guide; in the aftermath of the war we saw neither of the two major parties as the bastion of sensible policy.

A friend, Shirley Connors, showed us the way. Shirley was a Democratic stalwart, a precinct committeewoman, and a great expert on voters' unions in New York and Chicago. These unions informed their members about election issues. They published slates of recommended candidates. Under Shirley's tutelage, a few of us decided to form a nonpartisan slating organization for Monroe County. We would interview candidates in person with questions about their positions on issues we thought important. We would publish the results at our own expense to let other voters see what we had learned. If we could reach a consensus, we would also print a slate of recommended candidates. And with no apologies to Tammany Hall, we decided to call ourselves "Citizens for Good Government." A similar organization, separate from ours, focused on the I.U. campus vote. It was the Voters' Union, organized by Al Towell, Marilyn Schultz, Charlotte Zietlow, and others.

The details were crucial. Citizens for Good Government worked with teams of two interviewers, to counterbalance individual bias and to register more detail than a lone interviewer could do. Each team would report back to our whole group, which would try to reach agreement on each candidate in the hope of forming an entire slate. If we thought we needed more information, we would send the team back for more.

In those days there were few exceptions to the two-party system. If both candidates seemed worthy, we would endorse both. If no candidate seemed worthy, we would endorse no one. Sometimes we endorsed Democrats, sometimes Republicans. We tried to make it clear why we gave or withheld our endorsement. Above all, we were not reluctant to name names.

We had our critics. I recall a front-page, above-the-fold piece in the local newspaper with the claim that what we were doing was illegal. Democrats called us traitors, Republicans called us Democrats. Powerful critics notwithstanding, we seemed to fill a public need. Whether voters followed our advice, or we just happened to pick candidates the voters already favored, our slates had extraordinary success in the elections.

It took an enormous amount of work to cover an election properly. At our peak we had over 100 volunteers well known throughout the community, among them Shirley Connors, Kay Dinsmoor, Sue Martin, Sears Crowell and Leila Engel. We thought our work had helped improve the quality of both those who ran, and those who won public office. We thought it was worthwhile.

THE GOO GOOS DISBAND

In the early 1970s we sensed in local government a new climate of reform, transparency and media coverage that meant our day might be done. Some of us joined the government. Our volunteer force grew smaller. But we thought if we grew too small we could not continue to do the work properly. We grew uneasy with the possibility that our name and reputation might fall into the hands of a small partisan clique. Sue Martin sent a note around that sought to remind us about the parable of The Little Red Hen: If the other animals were going to let her do all of the work, they could not expect to share in the harvest.

We had agreed from the start that if the time came when it became too difficult to sustain our good work, we would rather disband than degrade the product. And that is what we decided to do at an evening meeting of about twenty-five members. We consoled ourselves with the thought that if the need should arise again, our model would be at hand.

To Citizens for Good Government and all of its Goo Goos, wherever they may be: Thanks and farewell.

CHAPTER 3

The Campaign Trail, Miles 1-3

I had a few close calls, but lost none of my ten city elections. I would be hard pressed to state any general rule about winning or losing, but it helped that I took none of the ten for granted.

My first election came in the summer of 1977, a City Council contest for the at-large seat vacated by Brian de St. Croix when he moved to another city. Interim replacements were made in such cases by vote of the City Council. The mayor would break

City Councilwoman Allison, 1979 (uncredited photo).

any tie vote. Councilman Jeff Richardson told me he wanted to nominate me. I replied by suggesting other candidates instead, but he insisted, with the support of his three fellow Democrats. I had no support among the four Republicans, who had crossed me off as a member of the American Civil Liberties Union, a dangerous radical or—most damning of all—a faculty wife.

Democratic Mayor Frank McCloskey, whom I had asked for his support, broke the impasse by voting in my favor. Afterwards Frank told me he would not have voted for me had I not asked for his vote in person and in so many words. Thus, "Never leave anything to chance" might be a corollary to "Never take an election for granted."

Second and third were the primary and final elections of 1979, which returned me to my seat on the City Council. Somewhere along the way the Republican members grew to accept me, and I served twice as council president.

As my name appeared more often in the newspaper, mystification spread about its pronunciation. I had long since learned to answer to all versions without complaint. "Tomilea" was interpreted variously as Tommy Lee, Tohmee Lee, Tahmeelia, or Tohmeelia. I was seldom called—correctly, in the opinion of my mother—Tom'-uh-lee, and still more seldom—correctly, in my own opinion—Tom-uh-lee'-uh.

My preferred name, "Tomi," was less puzzling. It often came out as Tammy, Tohmee or Tony, but more often correctly as Tah'-mee. Sometimes it was Bobby, from people who thought I had a boy's name but could not quite remember which one. To this day, little boys give me a second look to see if they heard right.

"Radosevich" seldom came up. Just for the record, my grandfather's version, the original, was Rad-oh'-suh-vich.

POLICE PRANKS

Few politicians are more political than firefighters or police. My serious schooling about that began as a member of the City Council when I and the mayor were up for reelection.

I had heard about a police faction hostile toward the mayor. Hostilities had peaked when he came down hard on some officers caught in flagrant misbehavior with prostitutes, such as sex in a police car parked in a stadium lot.

The lads meant to get even. They had already tried at a party out in the countryside, where someone gave the mayor a tip: A guest had some marijuana, and the police were on their way to make an embarrassing bust. Thanks to the timely tip, the mayor was gone when the police showed up.

Later he asked me to come along on a campaign visit to a bar that was supposedly a favorite hangout for gays. A friend of the mayor's who frequented the bar would introduce him; it would be a good chance to show a sympathetic face to gay voters. That night we had already attended another political gathering together, and he wanted company; would I come too?

I had my misgivings. It might seem odd for me, the housewife councilwoman with the sensible shoes, to be popping into a gay bar late at night. But he kept at it, and I went along.

As we mingled with the guests, what struck me was the ordinariness of both the bar and its clientele. So it came as a shock when the owner asked us to approach the street-side window to see a bunch of police cars lined up outside. The scene came straight from the movies. Several police cars, smack in the middle of the street, had parked in a semicircle with their headlights aimed at the door of the bar. We moved away from the window and considered the situation. The owner rushed over to tell us that the police might come inside and card everyone in the bar. Or, more likely, they would card a few guests and leave, in which case we would be spared any embarrassment if we would just move to the back room and quietly sit out the search.

We moved to the back room. When it became apparent that the police truly intended to card everyone, the owner suggested that we leave by a back door that led to the alley.

The moment we opened the door we met a police car parked in the alley. Undaunted, the mayor greeted its driver by name. Ever the gentleman, he introduced us: "Do you know Councilwoman Allison?" I thought he could have skipped the introduction, but we left without further ado. It was a good lesson in the role police could play in local politics.

CHAPTER 4

The Campaign Trail, Mile 4

I would have run for council again in 1983, had Frank Mc-Closkey not run for Congress. His surprise victory meant that Bloomington's Democratic precinct committee members would have to choose a new mayor in January, 1983. The occasion of their choice would become my fourth election, and one for the books. Anyone who sees my rise to mayor as some sort of inevitable progression should take a good look at that fourth election, starting with Joel Deckard's joust with the tree and Frank's subsequent move to Washington.

The horses dashed out of the gate upon Frank's election to Congress. Several friends suggested that I run, but I was far from the favorite, and not at all sure I wanted to run. True, the nest now had more room. Both daughters were grown, Devon in Los Angeles and Leigh at Indiana University. Jim kept telling me I knew the city inside out and would make the ideal mayor. All three urged me not to say "No." From California my mother phoned her advice: It was not a good time to be a mayor, she said.

I decided not to say "No."

I talked it over with close friends connected with the local party, and took soundings among the Democratic precinct committee members. Others, making similar explorations, decided to stay in or fold. By December my chances looked pretty good. I decided to run.

Twenty-six years later I ran into Mary Dieter, the *Louisville Courier-Journal* reporter who had covered the Bloomington beat during much of my political career. What leapt to her mind were the night and wee hours of January 4-5, 1983, when the precinct committee members met in City Hall to choose the new mayor. It took nearly five hours and eight ballots. The proceedings ended at 12:14 a.m. with a scene of four candidates, all smiles and unity, hands joined above their heads.[1] The other three were Al Towell, lawyer and city councilman; Patricia Gross, Frank's favored candidate and former executive secretary and city comptroller; and Tom O'Brien, inspector at Otis Elevator, a former county councilman.

Before the election Frank had declared neutrality, but with these pointed remarks to the newspaper. "McCloskey said he would try to work closely with the new mayor, 'whoever she is,' referring to interim mayoral candidates Patricia Gross and Tomi Allison. The other candidates are City Councilman Al Towell and former County Councilman Tom O'Brien."[2] Shortly before, the paper had noted the well known antipathy between McCloskey and Towell, who had supported the mayor's opponent, Charlotte Zietlow, in the Democratic primary election of 1975.[3]

County Democratic Chair Patricia Williams had called the Central Committee caucus for Tuesday, January 4, 7:30 p.m. It would be in the Council Chambers of the Municipal Building on Third Street—then City Hall, later home of the Police Department. She made it clear that personal attendance was required; no proxy vote would be allowed.

The meeting opened with a 45-minute discussion of ground rules that had supposedly been settled Monday, the day before. Most important, the winner must receive a majority vote, which meant 14 of the 26 Precinct Committee Members in attendance. Other rules concerned ties and elimination of candidates as the balloting progressed. Once the rules were settled, each candidate had ten minutes to speak, after which three persons could ask each candidate six questions. In the editorial opinion of the student newspaper, Pat Gross was the most articulate candidate.[4] Many participants disagreed with that opinion.

The first ballot, at 10:10 p.m., fell two short of a majority: Allison 12, Towell 9, Gross 5, and O'Brien 0. In the next three ballots I held steady at 12 votes, Towell and Gross varied between second and third place, and O'Brien received 0, as he did on every ballot.

On the fifth ballot I slipped from 12 to 11, and again on the sixth: Allison 10, Towell 10, Gross 6. After a 10-minute recess at 11:10 p.m., I recovered a little on the seventh ballot: Allison 11, Towell 10, Gross 5.

At that point the McCloskey forces thought it best to call it quits. Pat Gross and Tom O'Brien withdrew, and we had another recess. The eighth ballot results came in at 12:14 a.m. At the words "Allison 15," applause broke out and Bloomington had a new mayor.

A disappointed voter was heard to lament the outcome, which he thought had just cost him a $30,000 job with the city. (Many years later he obtained a lucrative city job in a subsequent administration.) Between votes there had been much discussion in the corridors of City Hall. It is just possible that some horse trading and arm twisting went on during those recesses, but I neither witnessed nor did any myself.

I think it would be a mistake to explain my victory in terms of a difference in policy among the candidates. There was no big difference in policy. There was no big difference in executive experience; we were all rookies. I think it was a matter of many small distinctions, weighed differently by a wide variety of voters. In my favor I would count the personal relations I had built up over many years of face-to-face work with volunteers on many social issues, large and small. As a member of City Council the city's department heads had come to know me well through my frequent visits to learn about their jobs and how City Council could help them in their duties to the city. None of them took part in the election, but they probably had some influence among those who did take part. I had not been a political threat to the outgoing mayor, whose favored candidate had entered the race rather late. As every ballot was cast in secret, the final outcome leaves much room for speculation.

Before the election Al Towell had said that he would run for mayor in the spring primary whatever the outcome of this election. Now he said he wasn't sure. He would wait and see how I did.

My husband Jim and our daughter Leigh took me to Nick's English Hut for a modest celebration. We had to cut it short in return for a little sleep before my first day in the office that morning. But word had traveled fast. As we filed out of Nick's, past a girl in a booth, she counted us off like sheep: "Which one is it? Him? Her? Her?"

On campus, the Sociology Department's bulletin board displayed a sign written by hand on departmental letterhead: "The Department of Sociology of I.U. proudly salutes our Mayor and our Bulletin Board Proclaims to the World: Our Mayor is a Sociology Major. Long may her honor serve." I must have told reporters about my major in sociology at Occidental.

CHAPTER 5

Starting Out

YOU LEARN SOMETHING EVERY DAY

Before I became mayor I had served on the City Council for five years, so I knew the council office in City Hall opened for business at 9 a.m.

On my first morning as mayor I walked downtown from my home, arrived at my office at 8:45 and found all of the City Hall employees already seated at their desks, hard at work. I found their dedication impressive. For the next few weeks I continued to arrive at my office a few minutes before 9 a.m., and continued to find all employees in their places and already at work.

I found this so remarkable that I finally mentioned it to a staffer who had been at City Hall for several years. "It's really impressive. When I come in I see no last minute rush to get to work on time, no stragglers, no flurry to get set up for work. They are already here, ready to go to work."

She gave me a long, thoughtful look. "Maybe that's because City Hall opens for business at 8 a.m., not 9."

From then on I came to my office around 7:45 a.m. And I noticed that as 8 a.m. drew near there was often a last-minute rush to get to work on time, a flurry to set up and a few stragglers.

They were good, but they were human. And I still had a lot to learn about City Hall.

PLANS

I had not managed a city before, but thought I knew what needed to be done.

We would campaign on major improvements in parks and thoroughfares. We needed more fire stations. We needed more space for city offices, and almost certainly a new city hall. We had to revitalize the downtown, preserve and enhance neighborhoods, and improve livability for all. We had to create a new master plan to guide future growth of the city. We had to upgrade our utilities infrastructure, especially water and sewer. I had run for mayor because I wanted to do all of these things.

These abundant city needs required an ambitious, vigorous city administration. We would have to have money from new sources, careful planning, and cooperation among city departments.

At a meeting with the key department heads, we agreed on a strategy that began with priorities. Road and park improvements would come first, because they were what the public cared about most. Next would come fire stations, for their vital importance to city safety. Downtown would come next, because we could start the work of revitalization relatively soon, with a relatively modest outlay. As City Utilities had their own income, they could begin improvements within their annual budget. As for the new master plan, it seemed sensible to begin with the less developed areas of the city.

We agreed on a timetable for these projects with the understanding that the responsibility for each part of our overall task would lie with the department head assigned to that part. It would be my job to clear the way politically for each part of the task.

The Comptroller, the Corporate Counsel, the Deputy Mayor, and the Director of Public Works became known as "The A-team." Every week the team met to review our progress and our problems. Every year, timetable in hand, we mapped out what remained to be done. To help us keep track of our accomplishments, Pat Patterson, the head of Public Works, gave me a little brown jar labeled "Promises Kept." As we completed each task, I denoted the event on a slip of paper that I deposited in the jar. Pat's little jar, nearly full, is my prized A-team relic.

GUM

Before I entered public service I had no true appreciation of the difference between life in the eye of the public and life as a private citizen. Gum is a good example.

For as long as I can remember I have loved to chew gum. But when I became mayor I knew I would have to choose my gum-chewing opportunities with great care, because chewing gum was simply not mayoral.

The library had asked me to make a television promotion for Library Week. As I walked from City Hall to the library, where the local access station would film the program, I happily chomped away as I reminded myself that I would have to ditch the gum before I came within range of the camera.

When I arrived I found everything nicely informal; it would be a candid live broadcast of me and the staff chatting about the glories of books. We got right down to it. Caught up in the spirit of casual realism, I forgot about the gum.

In the few minutes it took me to walk back to City Hall an elderly lady in the television audience had phoned my office with a suggestion. She thought the mayor should set a better example, and not chew gum in public. Of course I agreed, but still forgot from time to time to stow my gum away, and often heard about my lapses.

Some do better than others at public deportment. Did Margaret Thatcher chew gum? Golda Meir? Probably not. At least not on camera.

I had a lot to learn about public complaints.

When the head of the gas company walked into my office for his appointment and set a tape recorder on my desk, I had to wonder what I might be in for. It was an election year. The national news was full of sting operations with politicians and tape-recorded evidence. A city employee with an illegal hookup had been caught stealing city electricity. What might the man from the gas company have in mind?

I had made a habit of visiting local business leaders just to get to know them and hear any concerns about city government. This man was a newcomer, a stranger who had scheduled an appointment with no stated subject. I was on edge.

He turned on the tape recorder, played it a few seconds, and turned it off. "Did you hear that?"

"Yes," I said.

He played a few more seconds. "Did you hear that?"

"Yes."

"What do you think it was?"

It had sounded to me like the faint crow of a rooster off in the distance.

"Yes," he said, "that is exactly what it is." The gas man lived in city surroundings all right, but not actually in the city. A jurisdictional map would have shown that his apartment sat on a kind of small island, inside the city but not yet annexed by the city, and therefore still under county control. Eventually the city did annex that island, but at that time the jurisdiction remained in Monroe County. Thus, the gas man shared his island with a Monroe County rooster that deprived him of his sleep by crowing every morning, very early, as roosters do. The man lay awake all night, waiting for the rooster to herald the early dawn.

His work had begun to suffer. His appeal to the rooster's owner had not helped. The city's animal control officer had no jurisdiction over a county rooster, but promised to intercede as a courtesy. The crowing had continued.

The gas man appealed to county government, but there were no laws against the crowing of county roosters.

At last he came to me. Could the city stop this public nuisance?

I was sorry, but the city could do nothing for his predicament. I offered a few sympathetic suggestions, and that was that.

A few weeks later at a public gathering I asked about his rooster problem. "It's gone," he said. The rooster had left the neighborhood. According to a neighbor, a mysterious van had appeared early one morning. Its driver got out, grabbed the rooster and drove away. The rooster had not been heard of since.

Still later I met a representative of Opportunity House, a nonprofit used-clothing store. The store had once kept a collection box near the center of the city, but had found it necessary to get rid of it. "You should see what people put there!" A volunteer had stopped to make a collection from the box, and swore never to make another. "What do you suppose he found? Someone had put a live rooster into that box. Can you imagine!"

Indeed I could. I could even imagine how it might have gotten there.

THE NIGHT THE PRINCESS FELL DOWN

It's funny how people remember you. Over twenty years after the collapse of a downtown building, a young man recalled my response as the sign of my ability to run the city.

It happened on a hot, humid night when I had been mayor for only a few months. My husband suggested that we go to the store, buy something cold and spend a quiet Friday evening at home.

On the way home we noticed a commotion near the square with police cars and fire engines. We parked and walked a couple of blocks to the disturbance, already the center of a large crowd. On Sixth, a little east of Walnut, was a big pile of brick and other assorted rubble that could be none other than the chaotic mess of a large building fallen apart. The area had already been taped off, but there was much milling about and no one in charge. I found out what I could, and started to weigh the alternatives.

All we knew was that an abandoned movie theater called The Princess, located on Walnut, had collapsed in part and taken with it some structures on its nearest side street. Some of the debris filled an alley onto Sixth. Nobody knew the extent of the damage or when the rest of the building might fall. Was anyone inside? Was anyone in the alley, trapped beneath the wreckage? We saw that the falling rubble had crushed a classic treasure parked on the north side of Sixth, a 1957 Chevrolet convertible.

I huddled with the City Attorney, the Director of Public Works, and the Fire Chief. We thought it would not be safe to clear any wreckage until we could move some heavy beams that threatened the stability of the site. The job would require equipment the city did not have. We thought of Harold Weddle, the public-minded owner of a construction company who could deploy cranes and other such gear with the necessary expertise.

Weddle was not at home, but we soon reached him at his weekend retreat on the lake. The crowd waxed and waned throughout the several hours it took to sort things out. About 3 a.m. we saw there was nothing more to do until the light of day, and the two of us went home.

Nobody was hurt. The probable cause of the collapse was a structure that weakened when one of the building's owners, who enjoyed pounding its inside walls with a sledge hammer, accidentally damaged a load-bearing member.

Years later, when I left the Mayor's office I resumed my old ways as a civic volunteer. I worked once a week at Opportunity House, a nonprofit resale business whose proceeds went to the support of a child care center. During one of my stints at the cash register, some 21 years after the fall of the Princess Theater,

I overheard a young man praising my service as mayor. I could not figure out who he was.

When I got the chance, I asked whether he had ever worked for the city. "No," he said. Years ago, as a boy tuned to the radio one evening he heard that the Princess Theater had just collapsed. He jumped on his bike, rode a few miles to the scene, stayed several hours, and took careful note of how I had gone right in and taken charge of the emergency. He decided then and there that I was all right, and the city was in good hands.

Others had mentioned having seen me the night the Princess fell down. Many people were there, but I was only dimly conscious of the crowd. What I remember best is the care we took to cause no further damage, and the relief I felt when I learned that no one had been injured. The political message from the boy on the bike was that acts leave deeper marks than speeches.

MOM

I was only 49 when I became Mayor, but my hair had already been gray for years. I sometimes thought to change it, but my husband insisted that he liked it just the way it was. And it was common knowledge at City Hall that I had two daughters, then in their twenties, whom I had raised with a fairly firm hand. My choice of clothing was matronly, and a reporter once called my shoes "sensible"—a charge that earned her the enmity of my loyal staff, although the allegation had some merit. Still, it came as a surprise when, a couple of years into the job, I learned that the staff called me "Mom" behind my back. It was "Better not let Mom know you're going to handle it that way," or "Better check with Mom first," or "Let's see what Mom thinks about that."

I was not at all annoyed. I was pleased and honored to have my staff think of me as "Mom," as I considered that to be a job of the highest responsibility.

MADAME MAYOR [SIC]

Any discussion of local color would have to include Ross Allen. Allen was a faculty member of the I.U. School of Music, eternal radio host of "Sunday Opera," and master of gossip and anecdote in the musical arts community. He looked as if he had just stepped out of a Dickens novel.

Our paths crossed as I was out for a stroll one evening on the downtown square. Ignoring my companions, he greeted me in French with an extravagant bow and flourish: "Ah! Madame Mayor, en promenade!"

POT HOLE, TWELVE O'CLOCK HIGH

Already absorbed in city matters as a council member, I grew more so as mayor. My friends' responses to my absorption ranged from humorous to tolerant.

I enjoyed walking, but seldom got the chance to walk to work because the day's schedule usually called for me to drive some distance on city business. When I did walk, I always seemed to spot something that needed to be handled. If I saw some uncollected trash I would make a note. If I saw a big broken limb on a tree plot, a pot hole in the street or a broken curb or sidewalk, I would make a note. When I arrived at City Hall my notes would go to the appropriate department heads for action.

One morning the staffers heard that I had taken a new route on my walk to work. "Uh-oh," said the man at Public Works. "Watch out; the Mayor is widening her range." They joked about an "Adopt-a-Pothole" program.

My husband gave me a small tape recorder to make notes as I drove around town. He never got used to that sudden detached voice from the other seat: "Pot hole at X and Y. Broken curb at P and Q. Trash heap in the 1200 block of Z, west side of the street."

Later I established a paper trail for citizen complaints that came into City Hall by telephone. The person who took the call had to fill out a card that listed the particulars: When the call had come in, what it was about, and when and how it was taken care of. I examined these cards regularly, to make sure the complaints had been handled well.

Recently I opened an old box and found that small tape recorder, its silvery finish dull, dinged and scratched. I put it back in the box. No doubt the battery was dead.

NEW KID AT THE ROUND TABLE

As mayor I often attended the Southern Mayors' Round Table. There you would meet mayors and their staff members from towns south of Indianapolis, and merchants with various city goods and services for sale. At my first meeting the host city was Jasper. After lunch in a private dining room our host mayor invited us to a back room meeting of mayors only. It seemed that our group was faced with a problem of some delicacy. It seemed too that I had made the problem even more delicate, both as the only female there, and as a new mayor whom none of them knew.

One of us had asked for advice from the group. One of this mayor's policemen had been sent out alone to interview the witness to a crime. The witness, a young lady, made a sexual overture to the officer. The officer accepted, and the lady was indiscreet. She talked. Soon the affair became common knowledge, and a problem for our mayor. What should he do?

Much sage advice was offered and discussed, probably in language more refined than usual. At last we came around to the question of action. As the officer was still in his probationary period, it would not be hard to fire him if that was what he deserved. But did he deserve an outright dismissal, or only a reprimand? After all, the sex had been consensual. What should be done?

I spoke up for the first time and offered a suggestion. "I think he should be dismissed. His offense?" I paused for effect. "Being out of uniform while still on duty."

Nobody laughed. As these mayors were plainly not ready for levity, I got serious. "Look, he's in his probationary period. His behavior shows that he is not the kind of person you want in your police department. You should fire him."

And that was the group consensus.

CHAPTER 6

Denver Smith

Denver Smith came home for Monday lunch, a sandwich at his Henderson Courts apartment. Ten days ago he and Cynequa, married for thirteen months, had become the parents of daughter Ambrosia. He kissed them goodbye and never came back, killed that afternoon by police gunfire. The date was September 12, 1983. I had been mayor for nine months, and faced reelection seven weeks hence.

A high school football star, Denver Smith had come to I.U. from Dayton, Ohio, in 1978, on a full scholarship. His play at middle guard improved steadily. A 1981 press guide described him as a 5'-11" middle guard, the team's strongest player, good at rushing the passer. A senior-year injury gave him an extra year of eligibility, a final season of play in all eleven games. He had returned to finish his degree in physical education.

Some who knew him well—professors, his former coach, Lee Corso—would later describe his behavior that Monday as unusual, bizarre, or confrontational. Around 3 p.m., about a mile from his home, he had stopped traffic on South Henderson Street, near the Black Lumber Company. City employees Tim Morris and Mike Atkins told how the side mirror of their truck had brushed him as he tried to flag them into the opposite lane.

Morris said, "His eyes were real big, like he was mad about something."

He was scaring motorists with what they called variously a "tire iron," "jack handle," "tire tool" or "hub cap removal tool." It was actually a jack handle, one quarter inch in diameter, 18 to 20 inches long when folded and about three feet long unfolded.[1] Edward Jarrels had a CB radio in his truck. Smith approached him at an intersection and tried to flag him to the right. Jarrels thought he was flag man on a city work crew. Smith unfolded his jack handle, locked it into one piece and laid it across Jarrels' truck. When Jarrels reached for his CB radio, Smith warned him: "When you do that, I'm going to die and you're going to die." An off-duty I.U. policeman, Henry Miller, saw the encounter with Jarrels and called the Bloomington police.[2, 3]

It was a typical September day in Indiana, hot and humid. Three Bloomington police officers responded to reports of a big, shirtless black man threatening motorists with a jack handle. Smith weighed about 270 pounds and was an avid user of the I.U. weight room. He had held its bench-press record of 430 pounds.[4] When the police caught up with him he was south of Black Lumber, behind a storage shed at the Service Control Center, a municipal facility.

First to arrive was sergeant Steve Sharp, the senior officer on the scene. Sharp was a Vietnam combat veteran, Green Beret, college graduate, among the top twenty and president of his class at the police academy. He had been on the Bloomington force for seven years, and was the firearms instructor. Two more officers soon joined him, Randall Keller and Jimmy Ratcliff, both military veterans. Keller, with the Bloomington police for nearly six months, was still in his probationary period, but he had also served in the military police, as a security guard at Crane Naval Weapons Support Center, and as a Monroe County sheriff's deputy. Ratcliff, an army Vietnam veteran, had graduated from

Ball State, was third in Sharp's academy class and a deputy town marshal before he joined the Bloomington police department and became its night stick instructor.

Sharp said he approached Smith and asked him to put down the jack handle. Smith walked toward him, said "I am you father" and raised the handle. Sharp grabbed the jack handle and Smith struck him in the face with his left fist. Sharp's forehead still bore the scars from that blow years later.

The leather holster on Sharp's gun belt carried a revolver, a Colt Python 357 Magnum. Smith grabbed the pistol, tearing it out of the holster with such force that the holster's seams were ripped apart from top to bottom.

When Keller and Ratcliff appeared they saw an officer down, and his assailant. Ratcliff used his night stick to get Smith away from Sharp, but threw it down when he saw the gun in Smith's hand. Keller saw the two officers' lives in danger, and shot Smith twice in the lower back, ineffectually. Keller then used his revolver as a club, striking Smith in the head three times, again ineffectually.[5] As to the gun in Smith's hand, Keller testified later that he could see Ratcliff holding its cylinder, keeping the chamber from turning and letting it fire. He saw Smith's finger firm on the trigger. Had Ratcliff lost his grip on the cylinder, " . . . that would have been it."[6] Ratcliff fired the two final shots that brought Smith down. The fatal fourth shot severed Smith's aorta. The weapon was Sharp's pistol, which Ratcliff had wrested from Smith.

In Sharp's recall of the confusion of that ninety-second struggle, he took blows from Smith's fists and a night stick. When he heard gunshots he was beneath Smith and the officers. The next thing he knew, he was lying on his back against the building. Smith also lay on his back, hands above his chest. Four officers, their guns drawn, stood around Sharp in a semicircle.

Sharp radioed for an ambulance: "We have a shooting." But Smith was already dead.[7] A newspaper photograph in black and white, taken soon after the shooting, shows the somber Sharp and detective James Haverstock walking away from the scene. Dark spatters appear on Sharp's face and uniform.

I was on some official errand at Bloomington North High School when a phone call came in. There had been a police shooting. I must go straight to the police department. There I found the chief and the city attorney, who briefed me as best they could. Reverend Ernest Butler soon came forward, an old friend and the preeminent leader of the black community. Reverend Butler immediately offered to go with me to visit the widow, Cynequa Smith, in her apartment to offer our condolences.

The police launched an internal investigation by its Police Advisory Board: Chief Phil Riley, Deputy Chief Gary Clendenning, and the three shift captains. The officers involved would not return to duty until the board had met.[8]

Smith was buried in Gary on Saturday, September 17, in the Oak Hill Cemetery.[9]

After a six-day inquiry, the Police Advisory Board announced its conclusion on September 20: The officers involved in the shooting had acted within applicable police regulations. The board requested further investigation by the City Board of Public Safety, a civilian group appointed by the mayor.

At that time I chose to expand my safety board temporarily to five with two additional appointments, both from the black community. One was John McCluskey, an I.U. professor of Afro-American Studies and a former Harvard quarterback. The other was Jim Butler, production director of WTTV, Bloomington, son of Reverend Ernest Butler. They joined the three regular members: Reverend Ronald Liesmann; Phyllis Trinkle, Community Action Program Director; and I.U. Law School professor Patrick Baude.

Some citizens were quick to oppose the Police Advisory Board. Among them was Tavis Smiley, Director of Minority Concerns for the I.U. Student Association, and later a television celebrity. He thought the police, poorly attuned to the value of human life, had used excessive force because of Smith's race. Smiley thought that differences between black and other cultures engendered white ignorance of black dialect, the cause of provocative language from officer Sharp. Had Sharp addressed him properly, Smith might still be alive.[10] Two weeks later Smiley changed his mind. He did not think the shooting was racially motivated, and he called for an investigation into its justifiability. He was on his way to Atlanta to speak at a Christian Student Leadership Conference, where he intended to give an unbiased account of facts reported by the police and the county coroner, and reactions by the I.U. community and black students.[11]

At the Smiley press conference it was noted that the Black Student Union planned a Saturday march from the Black Culture Center to Memorial Stadium. Mayor Tomi Allison and Police Chief Phil Riley had been invited to attend and answer questions at the stadium. I did attend—not with the chief, but with my assistant, John Langley, and my 24-year-old daughter, Devon, who had spent the summer helping with my campaign.

We met the marchers, about one hundred, in a tent outside the stadium. According to a report the following Monday,[12] I shared the marchers' concern, shock and bewilderment. I added that the city's duty now was to investigate carefully and thoroughly, with a citizen review. An accompanying photo shows the crowd pressed closely about me, apparently attentive and orderly, as I listen, serious and intent, to a mike-holding questioner. My daughter sensed a physical threat from the crowd, but I did not; perhaps I was more accustomed to such pressures.

The City Board of Public Safety began its three public hearings on Monday, September 26. All took place in the City Council Chamber, and typically attracted a full-house audience of about one hundred. All of the hearings started at 5:30 p.m., a time convenient for public attendance.

The first one featured over seven hours of testimony, into the early morning. Its main witnesses were the five detectives who

Mayor Allison with student marchers (J. D. Scott, Indiana Daily Student, *September 26, 1983)*

investigated the shooting. A reporter described the audience as mostly orderly, with occasional jeers or cheers in response to testimony. Board President Baude called frequent impromptu executive sessions to solicit directions from the other board members. He managed the proceedings by confining the crowd to written questions, which he put to witnesses selectively.

The second hearing, on Tuesday, was supposed to feature public testimony by the officers directly involved in the fight. However, their public appearance had been canceled because of arguments on Monday by Attorney Lawrence Brodeur on behalf of the officers. Brodeur threatened to take the board to court if it compelled those officers to appear. He argued that their appearance in this hostile public environment would focus attention on them, not on the issue at hand; moreover, all of their previous testimony had already been made public. As a result, the board heard their testimony in private session. Charlie Brown, one of two black officers in the police department, testified that he thought there was no racial motivation in the shooting. The board met with the coroner to view photos of the body.

The third hearing, on Wednesday, began with public testimony from the final witnesses—about twenty in all three hearings. President Baude then opened the meeting for several hours of general comment. The public comment was mostly critical of the police and the board. The police were called unprofessional, improperly equipped, under-trained, perjurious, slanderous, conspiratorial, inconsistent in their testimony, brutal, and racially discriminatory. The board was called superficial in its investigation, and excessively genteel in its handling of witnesses.[13]

I sat through all of the public hearings. Many of the critical comments were not about Bloomington police, but the police where the critics had lived before they moved to Bloomington.

I thought local news media did a fairly good job in their coverage of this complex, tragic story; with some exceptions they were complete, accurate and fair. Some out-of-town media were deplorable. Newspapers in Gary and Ohio printed sensational misinformation, and some radio broadcasts were appalling. It was my first serious personal encounter with counterfeit journalism—inflammatory guff passed off as daring reportage.

As the local investigations drew to a close the community formed three clusters of opinion. The two most apparent ones were citizens who accepted the findings after listening to the facts, and those who readily rejected them. The latter thought the internal police investigation a farcical whitewash because the police would always close ranks and protect their own with a coverup. They thought the civilian Board of Public Safety meant well, but its investigation seemed naive, superficial, or timid.

Police formed the third cluster, mostly out of public view. They thought I had deserted them by exposing them to criticism in the public hearings conducted by the Board of Public Safety. My actual reason for making the hearings so transparent was to spare the police from the long, bitter rancor of a suspicious public. In the short term, the hearings hurt. But I had already seen that worried citizens had come to believe that their police had acted properly.

On the advice of Chief Riley I had a talk with his resentful, demoralized officers who felt abandoned. I told them how proud I was of our good, professional police force. I had stood behind them all the way, and would continue to do so. They accepted my message. Many years later, after I was out of office, one of the involved officers approached me and expressed his appreciation, for which I thanked him. Even then his expression of gratitude gave me a lift.

AUTOPSY

A forensic pathologist, Dr. John Pless, Monroe County Coroner, had done Smith's autopsy. Dr. Pless was educated at I.U. and its School of Medicine, and had come to national attention three years earlier as one of a panel of six experts who identified Clarence Roberts as the victim of a fire. In 1980 a weekend blaze had burned a house in Nashville, a small town a few miles from Bloomington. The identification made news because Pless had already declared the same man dead in another Nashville fire ten years before. However, that 1970 fire had produced conflicting testimony as to the identity of the victim. Pless himself said that he had not been 100% certain about his earlier identification. The doubt proved well advised. Shortly before the second blaze, a court upheld the insurance companies' denial of Mrs. Roberts' claim of widowhood. This time Pless was certain: Clarence Roberts had surely died in the 1980 fire.[14]

His examination of Smith's urine revealed marijuana use within thirty days, but no other drugs or alcohol. A brain scan showed no causal abnormality, although Pless had thought on first examination of the scan that there might be some such abnormality. He had referred then to the brain as having a thickened membrane and a slight swelling. Many blood vessels were congested, and some had evidently hemorrhaged.[15]

Pless described the body as supremely well muscled. Some observers suspected that Smith might have used steroids to increase muscle mass in a try for a professional football career, but no test for steroids was conducted. Pless explained the omission as an oversight because he had assumed that the state toxicology lab would screen the urine sample for steroids, or send it elsewhere for such testing, but it did not. (At that time the University of California at Los Angeles had the only lab in the country that did such testing.)

Four years later, in 1987, Pless' pathology lab had its own such facility for use in the Indianapolis Pan American Games. He wanted to retest Smith's urine specimen, but found that it had not been preserved. By then "steroid rage" was well documented, its symptoms consistent with Smith's behavior on the day of his death (aggressiveness, distractibility, violent paranoid defensiveness). In 1988 another medical witness, an expert on athletic abuse of anabolic steroids, testified that Smith was a user at the time of his death. Dr. William Taylor based his opinion on health records, weight training reports, photos of the body and sworn police accounts of the fight. He thought Smith had used steroids for at least six years; his muscle mass and strength were unique to steroid users. (More recent understanding of drug interactions with brain injuries from football concussions also seems pertinent.)

Nevertheless, the question of steroid involvement remains open. Friends, family and coaches said they knew of no such use. Long afterward law professor Patrick Baude still regretted the failure to test for steroids, as such testing might have cleared up the mystery of Smith's uncharacteristic behavior. Officer Charlie Brown attended the autopsy, where he noted the impressive musculature and wondered about steroid use. " . . . in hindsight, I wonder why they did not look into that. But back in those days,

I think there was knowledge that steroids were being passed around, and a lot of the football programs looked the other way."[16]

Soon after his role in the Denver Smith case Dr. Pless was appointed to the faculty of the I.U. School of Medicine in Indianapolis. He served that community as Chief Forensic Pathologist for Indianapolis/Marion County, and retired from the medical school as the Clyde G. Culbertson Professor Emeritus of Pathology and Laboratory Medicine.

OFFICIAL FINDINGS

On November 1, 1983, the Bloomington Board of Public Safety released its unanimous report. Liesmann, president in the wake of Baude's resignation from the board, read the four-page report verbatim. The officers had acted properly in their confrontation with Smith, within both the legal provisions of Indiana code and police department rules and regulations. They had not provoked him in any way, had intended no bodily injury, and had seen no time in the struggle when it was reasonable to withdraw and communicate.

There were seven areas of future concern. First, the board would review police rules and regulations about the use of force, firearms and other equipment.

Second, the board would encourage the city to upgrade police training in how to deal with the emotionally disturbed, defensive tactics and weapon retention, and human and community relations; the training should employ minority instructors.

Third, the board would encourage the city to expand the force from 58 to 64, with minority hiring if possible.

Fourth, the board would encourage press and officials to discuss ways to obtain accurate and timely press releases.

Fifth, the board would demand that every complaint against the police department for the next three months be processed meticulously.

Sixth, the board would demand that police department rules and regulations be on file for public inspection at police headquarters, the city clerk's office, and the public and I.U. libraries.

Seventh, the board would encourage members of the public to continue their interest in Public Safety Board activities and their attendance at meetings.

Attorney Barry Brown, the officers' spokesman, expressed their relief and gratitude for the confidence shown by the board and members of the community in letters to the editor and other such venues.

Clarence Gilliam, president of the Monroe County chapter of the National Association for the Advancement of Colored People, appreciated some aspects of the report, but was disappointed with its treatment of the issue of deadly force. Joseph Russell, the I.U. dean of Afro-American Studies, thought the report focused too narrowly on the struggle between Smith and the police. The day after the release of the report, Monroe County Prosecutor Ron Waicukauski said that he would not ask for a grand jury investigation because to do so would only prolong a fruitless ordeal.

The report's final draft had come on the day of its release, in the Public Safety Board's fourth private session. The board had spent about thirteen hours drafting the report since the last public hearing in September.

A few days later 15-30 I.U. students and city residents gathered outside City Hall to protest. Their demonstration lasted about an hour, and ended as they marched through the building with a chant, "Remember Denver Smith."[17]

The report angered members of the Southern Christian Leadership Conference. With Smith's mother, eight members from its chapter in Dayton, Smith's home town, traveled to Bloomington for a meeting moderated by Patricia Glenn, of the U.S. Justice Department's community relations division. The chapter vice president, Reverend William Smith (no relation), reportedly asked me for all of the information used in the city's investigation. "We came up here to let you know that we are not pleased, and we are going to establish our own investigation." Their probe might reinterview the officers, and consult the FBI.[18]

In another incident related to Smith's death seven citizens were forcibly removed when they disrupted a church ceremony in honor of Martin Luther King. It was a Sunday evening in January, 1984, at Reverend Ernie Butler's Second Baptist Church. I approached the podium to request a citywide observance of King's birthday. As I began to speak, the Denver Smith Committee, six whites and one black, gathered in the foyer began to sing "We Shall Overcome," and continued to sing for five minutes. When it became evident they did not intend to stop, the usher and several helpers pushed them outdoors. They had distributed fliers that urged those in attendance to rise and leave in an orderly manner when I began to speak. Rev. Butler had called them cowards for not signing the fliers, and asked them to leave before I began. He thought such a protest unfortunate at a celebration of the foremost advocate for patterns of change.[19]

THE COURT

In June, 1984, Cynequa Smith filed a wrongful death suit in the Federal District Court in Indianapolis. Defendants were the City of Bloomington, the Bloomington Police Department, the Bloomington Board of Public Safety and the officers directly involved. Three different investigations had already cleared the police of wrongdoing: The internal police report, the Bloomington Board of Public Safety report, and the report of a six-month study by the U.S. Department of Justice that found no civil rights violations. Her attorney, Richard Hailey, brushed them aside. Such investigations, he said, focused on criminal wrongdoing, not negligence, and there had been no trial and no lawsuit.

As two counts referred to violation of civil rights, the matter would fall under federal jurisdiction, not state. A third count claimed inadequate police training on the part of the city, the police department, and the board of public safety. A fourth count alleged negligence on the part of the officers in their attempt to arrest Denver Smith.[20, 21] (As reported in 1984[20] the counts numbered four, the sum was $5 million, and four officers were named as defendants. When the suit came to trial in 1988 the counts numbered three, the sum was $1.8 million, and only three officers were named as defendants: Sharp, Keller, and Ratcliff. After trial the judge in the case remarked that he could not understand why Sharp had been named as a defendant.)

Judge John Tinder presided over the trial in February, 1988, a $1.8 million wrongful death lawsuit. On the first day, before the proceedings began, the widow and her attorney declined an offer of $300,000. The three officers, approached by the insurance adjuster about settling out of court, declined. They thought the only way they could vindicate themselves was to testify in open court.[21] The trial took twelve days, with each side staging a long parade of witnesses. The six (white) jurors, three men and three women, took fourteen hours to deliberate on the evidence bearing on three counts: police negligence, police violations of civil rights, and city failure to train the police properly. They rejected all three counts unanimously.

The three officers expressed their relief. By then Sharp was the Bloomington police chief by mayoral appointment (and years later elected as Monroe County Sheriff). "I'm anxious," he said, "to get back to my job and move the department forward, beyond this."

Cynequa Smith was upset and angry, but not surprised. She thought the jury had given officers the go-ahead to use deadly force. The attorney who represented the city, Douglas King, heard a different message in the verdict: Officers had a right to self defense.

Richard Hailey, attorney for Cynequa Smith, said that the history of this particular court revealed a tolerance for police actions that he found unacceptable. However, he derived some satisfaction from the Bloomington Police Department's increase in training after the shooting. "Bloomington already has passed what I call the Denver Smith proposals—everything I pointed out in this trial, they have remedied. That makes us happy."[22]

In March Hailey filed a notice of appeal in the Seventh Circuit Court of Appeals in Chicago. He said the appeal would rest on technical grounds that involved the judge's instructions to the jury, and testimony by a physician with a suspended medical license. In May Hailey's office indicated that the appeal had been dropped.[23]

AFTERMATH

After the shooting Cynequa returned to Gary with Ambrosia; a few years later they moved to Illinois—Bartlett, a town near Chicago, where Cynequa got a job as an insurance adjuster. She remarried in 1999.

As Ambrosia approached college age someone recalled a promise. It was Bill Wiggins, a professor in the Department of African American and African Diaspora Studies. John Ryan, then university president, had promised to establish a scholarship fund for Ambrosia to attend I.U. Cynequa had forgotten all about it.

Wiggins went to work; the university kept the promise, and Ambrosia became an I.U. student. Interviewed in her junior year, 2003, she said, "It just worked out, and I love it here. A lot of the professors that are still here from back then, they hear my name and they approach me and talk to me about my dad and what happened. One time a lady I work with said she remembered my dad and thought really highly of him. That meant a lot."[24]

Cynequa told the reporter that she harbored no grudge against the officers, but still thought the shooting unnecessary. She recalled what Denver had told her: "You don't ever have to worry about anything because as long as I'm here, I will take care of you. But if anything happens to me, you are the one who will have to take care of Ambrosia." She would often return to those words in the years ahead as she strove to make a good life for their daughter.

CHAPTER 7

The Campaign Trail, Mile 6

Although Al Towell had said he might run, I had no Democratic opponent in my fifth election, the 1983 primary. That Fall I would face businessman Jack Morrison, a member of the City Council. In the Republican primary Morrison had defeated his two opponents, writer/educator Kent Owen and businessman Don Wagner.

I file my candidacy for Mayor, 1983; behind me, Martha Sims and Dick Schmaltz (photo uncredited, undated).

That sixth contest stands out as my first general election campaign for mayor. One novelty was expert advice. My files contain a solemn letter, marked "confidential," addressed to me as mayor. Dated April 29, 1983, it was actually aimed at the fall election, not the primary. Part of its gist follows.

I should not agree to debate my opponent, particularly if it be Mr. **REDACTED**, unless I had discussed the matter with the publicity committee. (Note: My opponent turned out to be someone other than Mr. **REDACTED**. Nevertheless, I did share at least one public platform—the Black Elks Lodge—with the formidable Mr. **REDACTED** and his two primary opponents. All of us survived.)

As to my image, I should always appear as chief executive of the city. I should appear composed and in control.

I should be fun, not arrogant.

I should appear to know what I wanted. I should establish a platform and announce it in my state of the city address.

I should be decisive. I should seek good advice, and only then take my stand.

I should avoid anger, as I tend not to respond well when angry.

I should always give the pro-corporate image. (What?!)

The letter also bowed to the hard financial realities. Bumper stickers should not be used, because of cost. For the same reason, T-shirts and buttons would be limited. (No frugal housewife could object to this one.)

Our funding must have exceeded expectations, because we did use bumper stickers after all. They had the same layout as my yard signs, buttons, and T-shirts: "Mayor Allison for Bloomington" in bright gold letters against a dark blue ground, like the state flag.

Bumper sticker used in subsequent elections.

Tomi Allison with Jack and Sue Martin (undated, uncredited photo).

No doubt Sue Martin helped greatly with the bumper sticker fund. She was my across-the-alley neighbor, my dear friend, and an early major contributor. Her loyal enthusiasm bubbled over in the newspaper: "I've never met anyone else who cared more about the well being of people. She really cares that Bloomington is a pleasant place to live, and she will work to see that it is the best place to live in the country. She has a wide-ranging curiosity and likes to talk to many different types of people. She is a kind person who is intensely interested in other people's concerns."[1]

I also received my first instruction in public speaking. Another neighbor, Moya Andrews, a professor of Speech Communication, kindly offered to film and evaluate a presentation.

After they saw the film, Moya and a colleague agreed that I compared very well with other local politicians, but needed to improve. I should work on my transitions; sometimes the next subject seemed to come out of the blue. I was good with humor, asides, stories, human interest examples and other spontaneous lines; audiences liked them, and I should use them at every opportunity. I should be more animated. I should ask my rhetorical questions more vigorously. My response content in Q & A was usually excellent. But I should watch out for vocalized pauses, those "uhs," and speed up my replies. That would come with practice and thorough preparation. In addressing differences with my opponent I should be more direct and less hesitant by just coming right out and contrasting what he and I have done. She offered valuable advice about makeup, color of clothing, and hair.

On May 7, soon after the primary, 28 Democratic candidates and leaders attended a lakeside retreat to brainstorm issues for the fall campaign. My publicity committee chair set the agenda, which included an important financial decision: Each person would buy his or her own lunch at the lakeside Inn of the Four Winds.

We split into four groups, each with its own leader. Each was to come up with two likely opposition issues, and two likely issues of our own. With Betty Rae Preus, my campaign coordinator, I circulated among the various discussions. When they were done, four spokespersons took a few minutes to report the groups' conclusions to the rest of us, and someone summarized the whole thing. All candidates for office stated campaign issues, and talked of a unified approach to their races and the mayor's.

Campaign contributions began to flow our way. In the end we raised and spent $31,393—nearly twice the amount my opponent reported, and apparently more than Frank McCloskey had spent on any of his three mayoral campaigns.

Betty Rae got hold of a campaign bible from NOW (National Organization of Women) that we used to organize my campaign. We set a detailed schedule of action from October 14 to November 8. My walking schedule would send me door to door in the company of appropriate city council candidates. For example, my notebook shows that on October 14-15-16 we were supposed to walk two precincts, B-18 and B-13.

It was our bright idea to have every walker carry blank postcards, addressed to me, for distribution as we went door to door. The card said:

Help us keep Bloomington an All-America city. I would appreciate hearing your comments, questions and concerns about City policies and programs. Please use this postcard or send a letter to me at the Municipal Building.

~ Tomi Allison, Mayor

We had a productive phone-calling schedule. From campaign headquarters each evening, 7:00 to 9:00, callers would target registered voters—Democrats and Independents—and ask if they planned to vote for Tomi Allison. We targeted these calls geographically, to let voters know when I would be walking in their neighborhood the next day. Followup calls on the eve of the election, reminding them to vote, would go to Democrats and voters who had indicated their support. The size of my volunteer force surprised the Democratic Central Committee. I attributed the big turnout to the years I had worked with volunteers on cause after cause. They truly powered our door to door campaign.

To the undecided, the un-phoneable, and to newly registered and absentee voters we mailed a comprehensive packet. It contained my campaign brochure, the central committee brochure, and a letter that stated my platform. We made sure that central committee literature drops included my literature, some of it specialized by area; for example, the west side drop had a special flyer from my office entitled "The Real West Side Story." We arranged for I.U. faculty to stuff faculty mail boxes. Students stuffed dormitory mail boxes.

We put out 600 yard signs, and made frequent radio and newspaper ads. We tried to have one or two letters to the editor published each week in the *Herald-Telephone* and the *Indiana Daily Student*. There were frequent news releases from City Hall, courtesy of Assistant Mayor John Langley and city department heads.

My daughter, Devon, organized the campaign campaign along similar lines in terms of precinct walks, mailings, literature drops, personal appearances, posters, flyers and group endorsements.

We circulated my schedule of appearances among City Hall employees so they could suggest useful engagements for any open dates. We called for volunteers to accompany me on my walks and my speaking or social engagements. (One young man in particular walked with me on every campaign; he said very little, but enjoyed my give and take with voters.)

We did not have enough money to conduct a real poll, but the paper printed the results of a Republican poll taken around the middle of September. It showed me leading Morrison, 53%-26%, with 21% undecided. My lead was not a matter of name recognition, as the poll showed us each with 80% name recognition.

What were the election issues? Lots of things came up: the PCB cleanup, west side redevelopment, landlord/tenant and town/gown relations, economic development, public transit. The Denver Smith shooting was a major event that had shocked and appalled the entire community, but proved not to be divisive politically. The Republicans really had only one issue, which they pushed very hard: Jack Morrison was a businessman, and I was only a faculty wife. How could I possibly run the city?

There were two answers that many found persuasive. First, I had already run the city for several months, since January. I had conducted its day to day business, and led it through a major crisis. Second, as Jack and I campaigned around town, often together, the voters could see then and there how we answered their questions about city matters. They could see for themselves what each of us knew about running the city.

The tenor of the election was friendly enough, but there were some sharp exchanges. For example, at a forum of the Greater Bloomington Chamber of Commerce, Morrison the businessman made the point that local government should be run as a business. In defense, I said, "We are a business. But the end product is not widgets, it's quality of life." I added that I was " . . . the lead entrepreneur seeking to maximize our investment—people." He tried to score points on a supposed lack of city-county cooperation—for example, between city and township fire departments. I replied that the city had been working on just such an agreement, but that Morrison would not know about it because " . . . he has never talked to his own fire chief about it."[2]

I preferred not to mix it up with Jack Morrison, but was ready to go if pressed, remembering that I "… tend not to respond well when angry." As elections go, it was relatively civil.

Four days before the election, the *Herald-Telephone* endorsed me.[3]

On November 8 the voters returned me to office by a landslide, 62.2% to 37.8% (7,361 to 4,464).

Mary Alice Dunlap had been Bloomington's first and only woman mayor, appointed to office by the outgoing mayor, Tom Lemon. She was defeated in her first general election, largely because of her gender. Her husband's nickname was "Chet," and the Republican mantra was "Get Chet out of the kitchen." I was the first woman to win the seat in a general election.

Election night, Devon, Tomilea, Leigh, and James Allison (photo Bloomington Herald-Telephone, *November 2, 1983)*

Later I would demonstrate that one could win without newspaper support. I also learned that a landslide counts only once.

THE MYSTERIOUS STRANGER

Late in the race, when he was running behind, Morrison asked for a private meeting, subject undisclosed but "very important."

In my office at City Hall he began with a story about some personal enemy or enemies who had fired a bullet through the window of his residence. The details were not too clear, but he was plainly worried. I asked whether he had reported the incident to the police. He had not.

Next up was his tale of an encounter with a stranger from the West Coast, a person who might have known me, a native Californian, in the days of my youth. With the air of a co-conspirator, he intimated that the stranger had claimed to know something about my past that I would find most embarrassing as a candidate for public office.

I tried not to smile. If there was anything in my past that could inflict a fatal wound on my political career, it would be news to me.

The tale continued. Morrison had refused the stranger's offer to sell his lethal information to him. Morrison thought this kind of mud slinging would be out of place in our campaigns. He would use no such information against me. The unspoken hint was that I, in turn, should use no such information against him. With that our bizarre interview ended, and the subject never surfaced again.

His elaborate attempt to keep me quiet was unnecessary, as I had no wish to use personal gossip against any political opponent.

My permanent policy about the slinging of political mud was reiterated when my campaign manager, Betty Rae Preus, returned from a seminar on campaign tactics conducted by the National Organization of Women, where candidates had been advised to use every bit of dirt they could dig up to the disadvantage of their opponents. Betty Rae felt certain that we should not and would not use that tactic. She was right.

THE LUNCH BUNCH

After the 1983 election I began to meet regularly, about once a month, with the women most helpful in my campaign. The Lunch Bunch—Pat Williams, Betty Rae Preus, Kay Dinsmoor,

Anabel Hopkins, "Bee" Stafford, Alice Tischler, Jean Cook, Pam Lohmann and Devonia Stein—provided an invaluable sounding board of bright, caring citizens, generous with advice and opinions. Those still with us as I write—all except Betty Rae, Kay, and "Bee"—continue to meet even now, still pretty free with advice and opinions, much as they were in the old days.

The Lunch Bunch *(Left to right, back row:* Betty Rae Preus, Devonia Stein, Anabel Hopkins, Jean Cook, and Pat Williams. *Middle row:* "Bee" Stafford, Tomi Allison, Alice Tischler's visiting daughter and grand-son, Laura and Daniel, and Alice Tischler. *Front row:* Kay Dinsmoor and Pam Lohmann. (photo circa 1995, uncredited.)

CHAPTER 8

PCBs and I

Polychlorinated biphenyls (PCBs) are an organic compound of one or two chlorine atoms attached to a biphenyl, a molecule made of two benzene rings. Their sole producer in North America, Monsanto, made them from 1930 until 1977, and sold them under the trade name "Aroclor." Westinghouse sold them as "Inerteen," and used them in Bloomington as an insulating fluid in the manufacture of capacitors. Although the industry had known of their toxicity since the 1930s, for many decades it continued to push hard for their use in safety equipment. PCBs easily penetrate the skin, and degrade only slowly unless subjected to high heat or catalysis. They bioaccumulate in animals—the body does not flush them out—and they stay in the food chain. They are a clear, viscous fluid, tasteless and odorless. In humans they are probably carcinogenic and can probably cause systemic poisoning, damage to the liver or nervous system, and irregular menstrual cycles. PCBs also can impair the immune response and cognitive development. Congress banned the domestic production of this toxin in 1977. But before that ban, PCBs had become Bloomington's biggest environmental problem, and remain so today.

From 1958 until 1977 the Westinghouse plant in Bloomington dumped capacitor rejects in landfills and junk yards, where individual scavengers in search of metal sometimes spilled the fluids onto the thirsty ground. In deliberate violation of its extant contract with the city concerning the disposal of hazardous waste, the plant made matters even worse by dumping PCB oil into drains that sent the fluid on for treatment as city sewage, where it became sludge. Unwittingly the McCloskey adminstration created several hundred PCB sites by giving such sludge to local farmers and gardeners. Altogether, the plant dumped over two million pounds of PCBs in Bloomington.

Outside the Westinghouse plant, the town slept mostly unaware of the spread of PCBs and the growing hazard to public health. All of that changed in 1975 when City Chemist Rick Peoples attended a conference where he happened to learn that the "Inerteen" in our sewers was another name for PCBs. He recognized the danger, came home, and sounded the alarm. City officials tested the pipes in question, found significant PCB contamination, and began the first cleanup efforts.

It soon became evident that the contamination was no trivial problem. When the Environmental Protection Agency (EPA) finds that a hazardous waste site is a particularly serious threat to public health, the agency places that site on its national priority list of Superfund sites. The EPA listed Lemon Lane and Neal's Landfill as Superfund sites in 1983. Bennett Stone Quarry joined them in 1984.

My PCB education began with the city's earliest cleanup efforts, when I was City Council president. If memory serves, it took the threat of a lawsuit to move a reluctant Westinghouse to cooperate with the city even when the cleanup chore seemed to require nothing more than the flushing out of a few sewer pipes. But as the true enormity of the contamination emerged, Westinghouse shrank from all cleanup responsibility. That was why, after much deliberation, city officials, led by Mayor Frank McCloskey, decided to sue Westinghouse.

The decision to sue was a big deal. Mayor McCloskey initiated a national search for the best legal talent for the job. He settled on a Chicago attorney, Joseph Karaganis, chosen for his reputation as an effective litigator against big business interests. Karaganis undertook to define the terms of an agreement. It was his novel notion to hammer out a deal that would give the city some local control over the terms of any cleanup.

Arduous negotiations produced an agreement at last among Mayor McCloskey's office, Westinghouse, EPA, and the Indiana Department of Environmental Management (IDEM). In 1982 McCloskey won election to the U.S. House of Representatives. Once I replaced him as mayor early in 1983, all that remained to put the agreement in place was a favorable vote by the City Council.

Later that year, when I ran in the November election, the PCB cleanup never emerged as a contentious political issue. It came up for City Council approval early in 1984, by which time we had conducted several public hearings to lay out the terms of the consent decree. But in a parallel development, a national environmental movement had turned against incineration as a method of disposal, and the mass media had given incineration very bad press. As a result, by the time they took up the consent decree, the members of City Council found the cleanup to be a hot, divisive issue. Public attendance at council meetings, normally low, overflowed the chamber that night. Public comment grew heated as the evening progressed. There were angry shouts as the vote drew near. Part of the crowd surged forward as the council attempted a roll call vote, and someone ripped a microphone from its socket. In the noisy melee President Pat Gross asked the council members to signify their votes by raising their hands. She stood on tiptoe to count, and the measure passed unanimously.

In his home across the alley my neighbor, Jack Martin, had watched the proceedings on television with a growing anger of his own. He switched off the set, marched down to City Hall and confronted a part of the mob that had asserted citizens' rights to part of the council chamber and a microphone. He said that if their claim was true, any citizen could make the same claim. With that, he demanded the microphone for himself.

In the aftermath of that tumultuous evening it was hard to communicate the extraordinary features of the agreement—called hereafter the "Consent Decree." To appreciate these features, one must first understand that EPA Superfund law made two important departures from traditional American law. Ironically, both of these departures can be traced to the influence of a distinguished I.U. professor of political science named Lynton Caldwell, the principal originator of the 1969 National Environmental Policy Act and the concept of environmental impact. First, the Superfund law asserted retroactive responsibility. Second, it did not require proof of malicious intent. This meant that the city was responsible for the cleanup even though its ownership of the site and the pollution of the site preceded the Superfund law, and even though the city did not pollute the site. Thus, the city must clean up Lemon Lane simply because the city owned the polluted Lemon Lane site. Given the city's meager resources, and the projected cost of the cleanup, on the order of $200 million, this feature of Superfund law loomed as the mother of all unfunded mandates. In addition, Superfund law gave all authority over the cleanup to federal and state agencies: the Environmental Protection Agency, and the Indiana Department of Environmental Management. Local government could not do as it pleased; it had to follow federal and state law.

The Consent Decree, as written by Karaganis, overturned those rules. First, in a colossal financial victory for Bloomington, it stipulated that Westinghouse, and not the city, would pay the cost of the cleanup. Second, the method of the cleanup would be subject to local control. That is, EPA, IDEM and Westinghouse agreed with the city that the Bloomington Utilities Service Board would have the final authority to say whether the safety of any proposed cleanup method was acceptable. Such local authority had never been granted before—and has not been granted since.

Opposition to the Consent Decree was usually framed as opposition to incineration as a means of disposal. This was not quite correct. Although the decree specified incineration, it also granted Westinghouse the right to use any other method permitted by EPA. The fly in the ointment was that any method used must meet the EPA permit standard—an exceptionally high standard, on the order of 99.99% free of PCBs. Years later I learned from federal EPA scientists that this high standard was established at a time when all PCB contamination was liquid, a form easily incinerated to 99.99% pure. The problem was much more difficult in Bloomington, where the PCBs, far from liquid, were mixed with all manner of landfill trash. Thus, a standard of purification formulated for liquid PCBs, and not for the trashy soup we had in Bloomington, made it extremely difficult to find a suitable means of disposal.

Local politics began to churn when PCBs appeared in Anderson Road Landfill, outside the city but inside Monroe County. We invited county officials to join the Consent Decree, and they expressed interest. Several informational meetings ensued, all attended by the county attorney and a County Commissioner acting as liaison for county government—specifically, for the three Commissioners and the five members of the County Council. All that remained was a favorable vote by the commissioners and council members. On the date the vote was to take place I visited the liaison to answer any last-minute questions or concerns about the decree, but there were none. The way seemed to be clear. And at the meeting that night, all but one of the eight county officials voted in favor of the decree. The one exception was the liaison, whose turn to vote came last. My political antenna detected a signal.

Nevertheless, a big majority had voted to join the Consent Decree. This meant that the county would not have to bring its own law suit, and Westinghouse would pay for the county land-fill cleanup.

New impediments cropped up. Before any incinerator could be built and put into operation, we had to find a suitable place to bury the ash. Our karst topography made suitable places scarce, but we finally found space near the north sewer treatment plant. However, the site proposal aroused the opposition of two nearby landowners with sufficient means to form and finance "The Coalition Opposed to PCB Ash in Monroe County, Indiana" (COPA). This group stoutly and loudly opposed incineration. Thanks to their congressman, COPA received a grant of $250,000 from the EPA, for private citizen oversight of the very same cleanup the very same congressman had engineered as Bloomington Mayor Frank McCloskey. To those familiar with the Consent Decree, this action may have seemed duplicative. Hadn't the decree itself already mandated citizen oversight by our municipal Utilities Service Board? This congressional action added one more layer of oversight, for four layers in all: Federal, state, municipal, and COPA. In addition, it fueled political opposition to the Consent Decree.

In the next election year, 1987, County Commissioner Charlotte Zietlow—the county liaison—ran against me in the Democratic primary on the PCB issue, and very nearly won. My margin of victory was razor thin, seventy-five votes. Newspaper articles in the runup to that election fired a constant barrage of publicity about other possible cleanup methods. As alternatives to incineration, the opposition proposed one magic bullet after another, each hawked by some expert advocate brought to town for the purpose. Alas, none of these methods had been designed to clean up PCBs mixed with tons of municipal trash. Nevertheless, each new alternative was launched with much ado, and eventually fizzled out with little notice when it could not meet EPA standards.

One of the salient questions concerned the toxicity of PCBs. Positions on this question ranged from "utterly lethal" to "utterly harmless." One advocate of the "utterly harmless" view was a physician whose political philosophy, in periodical newspaper ads, was about as far right as one could get in those days. At a meeting of the Rotary Club, after I had given a speech on possible cleanup methods, I stood at the podium for questions from the audience. The doctor raised his hand and said "Heck, those PCBs are nothing. Why, I would be willing to spread them on soda crackers and eat them!"

"Fine," I replied. "But it will take quite a while to dispose of them that way."

The doctor laughed. We both knew that the PCB trash would have covered a football field to the height of a 25-story building.

When we first began the cleanup process we were naive enough to suppose that if people only knew the facts, they would realize that the Consent Decree would ensure a safe cleanup. Acting on that supposition, we asked the EPA to dispatch their scientists to Bloomington to explain to our citizens how incineration could be made safe. In the public meetings that ensued it soon became clear that emotion usually trumped reason. In meeting after meeting the EPA pitched science to a public mostly immune to that kind of talk. Local media typically made no effort to weigh the credibility of experts.

At last I traveled to Washington, D.C., to explore with EPA scientists any promising new methods of PCB disposal that did not involve incineration. Their answer was unconditional: Because ours were so thoroughly mixed with landfill, incineration was the only way to release our PCBs from the landfill trash and destroy them. And the mix was enormous: I flashed that image of a megalith 25 stories high, its footprint a football field. They admitted that the effluent produced by incineration would require the most thorough scrubbing and monitoring. The scrubbing equipment would have to be kept in tip top condition. That was when I learned that the EPA permit standard, 99.99%, had been promulgated for liquids, not solid trash. I learned too that the EPA was not about to change that standard, for fear of the potential furor. They were anxious to avoid any impression of a relaxation of standards in response to outside pressure.

In the run-up to the next election, our PCB attorney suggested a possible way to defuse the cleanup issue. As a campaign message I should assure the public that "No Unsafe Incinerator Will Be Built In Bloomington." The Consent Decree gave us the power to make good on that promise. The message became headline news, and seemed to produce some calm.

I emphasized the point in my State of the City Address of February 6, 1991, when I took Westinghouse to task for its adherence to a defective design, the O'Connor incinerator. (As the O'Connor could not maintain a constant temperature, it could not achieve complete combustion of PCBs.) I made it clear that the city would simply reject such an incinerator, under the power conferred by the Consent Decree.

In the 1991 election cycle the cleanup was not a big issue. In the 1987 cycle all of our explanations of the safeguards inherent in the Consent Decree had fallen on deaf ears. Yet, those were much the same ears that heard, loud and clear, the simple message based on the decree: "No Unsafe Incinerator Will Be Built In Bloomington."

Our big pollution sites remain. They have not been cleaned up. They have only been capped, and their runoff treated. Three of the parties to the original cleanup agreement—EPA, the city, and IDEM—would never have accepted capping as a solution. The fourth party, Westinghouse, would have been happy simply to cap the mess it created. And that is our present state of affairs.

In light of our experience, I doubt that any community faced with our pollution problem would attempt to solve it with our kind of consent decree. Its fatal flaw was that the decree gave locals the power to stop any proposed method of disposal, but no power to dictate any particular method. The power to dictate possible methods remained in the federal hands of the EPA.

The PCB cleanup was the most difficult problem I faced during my thirteen years as mayor.

CHAPTER 9

The Campaign Trail, Miles 7-8

MILE 7

Around the state my friends in city government could hardly believe the news from Bloomington that spring night of 1987. As the evening dragged on, the early returns suggested that after five years as mayor I might be defeated in the May primary by a Democratic opponent. The opponent was Charlotte Zietlow, President, Monroe County Commissioners.

The big issue in that seventh election was the Consent Decree to govern PCB removal. It could have gone either way until the very last returns showed me ahead by 75 votes (2,570-2,495, or 50.7%). How had I managed to win?

According to the *Herald-Telephone*, "Allison . . . used a well-financed, well-organized campaign to counter Zietlow's straight-to-the-people approach. Democratic voters were targeted, delivered literature and telephoned by Allison's organization in an effort to get out the vote."[1] Actually, I campaigned the same way as always, door to door. However, in this particular election I spent most of my time standing on door steps explaining the value of the Consent Decree.

I explained the narrow margin to the reporter as an anti-incineration vote and referred to blurred media representations of the power of the EPA in choosing the method of disposal. I also mentioned blurred media representations of the value of the Consent Decree as a means of unique local control over the cleanup. I opined that the only way I might get the message across was to go door to door.

My opponent saw the results as a more general dissatisfaction with my administration's handling of basic services, street conditions, and PCB cleanup. She seemed surprised when reporters asked if she would support me in the fall election. "I've always supported the candidate of the Democratic Party."[2] I should note that our local Democratic Party never endorsed candidates in primary elections.

I adopted a new slogan for the fall general election: "Under no circumstances will I allow an unsafe incinerator to be built."

I declared my mind open to any practicable alternative to incineration, and I meant it. I traveled to Tucson to inspect an exciting new alternative that turned out to be impracticable for our particular cleanup. We heard of many such methods: exposure to sunlight; bacteria that thrived on PCBs. None of them panned out. The basic problem was that our PCB's were mixed with garbage.

Nevertheless, my espousal of the Consent Decree led some detractors to call me "Allison in Wonderland." I chose to take the name as an unintended compliment. Wasn't Alice the one rational creature in a land stocked with nuts—the Mad Hatter, the March Hare, the Cheshire Cat and the Queen of Hearts?

SCHOOL DAYS

I often visited schools to talk about government. It sometimes happened that the students themselves would illustrate the problems and potential of governance infused with emotion.

A fourth-grade teacher at University School invited me to talk about democracy. As I looked over the classroom I saw that a good half of the class consisted of foreign students from the Middle East. I already knew that it would be almost useless to address fourth-graders in abstract terms, so I decided to start off with a concrete example.

"I'm Queen Tomi. Because I'm Queen, everybody has to do as I say. And I have decided to issue a decree: From now on, only the girls get to go to school. The boys have to stay at home and learn to cook and sew." I paused, expecting to go on to discuss the differences between a dictatorship and a democracy, but the boys gave me no chance to go on. They lunged forward in their seats, talked and shouted all at the same time. They would not stand for any such rule. They would not obey. They would get a gun and shoot me.

I had an answer. "I'm the Queen, so I have a big army that has more and bigger guns than anything you could come up with. Besides, you really don't have to shoot me. We have a democracy, and in a democracy all you have to do if you don't like me is to vote me out of office." That calmed them down, and we went on to have a good discussion about democracies and dictatorships.

After class a delegation of four girls came up to talk with me. The natural leader of the group confided her career plans: "When I grow up, I'm going to be President."

I was invited to a class of preschoolers whose teacher had taken the opportunity of an election year to teach them first hand about candidates, campaigns and balloting. The class had chosen two candidates, a boy and a girl. The teacher had helped each candidate to come up with a platform and a big set of campaign promises frankly oriented toward fun: games at recess, pizza parties and the like. Each candidate took a turn with a toy microphone in front of the class and made a campaign speech, after which the election began, complete with a ballot box and ballots with photographs of the two candidates.

As the vote count proceeded the little girl came over to my tot-sized chair, leaned close to my ear, and admitted that she was worried that she might not win. Sure enough, the boy was elected president. All of the boys had voted for him, and some of the girls. The girl sighed: "I knew I shouldn't have promised that fingernail-painting party."

Maybe we could cheer her up. I said to the teacher that the class now had a president, but what about a vice president? Maybe the person who had come in second could be vice president. The grateful teacher grabbed the suggestion: If it was all right with the president, the girl could be vice president. That was just fine with the boy, so the two candidates went home happy. It wasn't altogether realistic, but it was a good way to break in a preschool politician.

WEDDINGS

I knew that ship captains could perform weddings, but it came as a surprise to learn that mayors could too. Normally I performed this service for nothing, but if a couple insisted I agreed to accept payment on condition that the money would go to the city Tree Fund as a contribution in their name.

Most of the time I performed the simple civil ceremony in my office with little ado. Usually speed and convenience were the order of the day, but couples sometimes made more exotic arrangements. Among the more memorable were the two who wanted to be married in a hot-air balloon in free flight. As I had already made one flight in a balloon from Bloomington to Spencer, their request did not seem so perilous or outlandish as most of us might think. As we boarded the balloon I noticed that the bride and groom were already quite merry, and the champagne they had brought on board seemed to keep their spirits high. As we floated across the countryside I did my duty, and when we landed in some farmer's field they landed as husband and wife.

A springtime wedding was attended by Morris dancers. We drove out to a university forest north of town, and I stood with the bride and groom in the middle of a moving circle of costumed dancers adorned with bells and ribbons.

Although the office weddings were not so exotic, some of them were memorable for other things. I often think of the bride who simply could not stop laughing as I tried to perform the ceremony. How could I get them married if all she could do was giggle? At last I fixed her with my beady-eyed school marm stare, told her to repeat after me, and led her phrase by phrase into the civil state of matrimony.

Many years since my last ceremony, couples still come up to me and say "Mayor Allison! Do you remember us? You married us, and here we are." I wish I truly remembered them more often than I do. It was one of the best parts of my job.

CONFUSION

A day in the Mayor's office could be pretty hectic. My appointment book might list office meetings with several different individuals on several different topics, staff meetings, a working lunch, and trips outside the office for public appearances at events scattered throughout or even outside the city. The calendar could be crowded, the notation terse: Luncheon speech at Rotary; Dinner at Crane; Interview Mr. X. It was easy to get confused.

More than once I found myself at a gathering waiting for a meal, a speech or a ceremony to begin, on the prior understanding that I was just a part of the crowd, and not a featured attraction. But as I stood listening to the swirl of conversation around me, the drift of the talk might lead me to think that in fact I was a featured attraction, and that I was expected to say or do something special. The nightmare would usually fade as the proceedings began, and I was seldom called upon for any major feat of improvisation.

However, I was not immune to confusion. I went to a lot of weddings when I was mayor, and it could be difficult to keep them straight. I recall a weekend calendar that listed the wedding of a friend's daughter at a church that I will call the "X Church." At the appointed time and place I took my seat on the bride's side, surrounded by familiar faces. In a small town almost any wedding crowd will have some familiar faces. But when the mother walked down the aisle, she was not the friend I expected. I must have gone to the wrong X Church!

I simulated a fit of coughing, left the building, got into my car and sped across town to the other X Church. I parked, hurried inside and sat down in back. I was just in time to see my friend's smiling daughter rushing up the aisle and out of the church with her new husband.

Things could get pretty hectic, but they usually worked out.

A NEW CITY LOGO

I wonder how many Bloomingtonians remember the old city logo. There may be more than one old logo, but the one I recall looked like Rutherford's planetary model of the atom, a nucleus at the center of several rings. It did not seem to make much sense as Bloomington's city logo, and I had heard quite a lot of puzzled, critical comment about that. Far from the most crucial problem to come across my desk, it was still quite important to some citizens, and looked as if it might be fun to resolve.

In 1986 we staged a new-logo contest. The winner was Tim Mayer, a member of our city council.

Tim's winning design resembled dark blue paper cutouts on a white background. At the center was a white square oriented as a baseball diamond. Arranged around the white diamond were eight blue figures that some saw as a flock of birds, others as a flight of arrows headed toward the diamond. Some saw a patchwork quilt, some a silhouette of Batman.

My verbal description of Tim's handsome new logo is plainly inadequate, but may at least arouse some curiosity. Were it not protected by copyright I might print the logo here for all to see, but the Internet renders that unnecessary. And you can always visit City Hall and see our popular Rorschach of a logo on the wall of City Council Chambers.

THE FAMILY AIRPLANE

It did not take long for local politics to finger my family life. This story needs to be told by Jim.

CENSOR

In 1982, before Tomi became mayor, I scraped together enough cash, $6,500, to buy an airplane. In those days, that was pretty much the rock bottom price for an airplane.

Why was it so cheap? Several reasons. It was 36 years old. With a full load of gas it could carry the pilot and one passenger if both traveled light. It cruised at a leisurely 95 miles per hour on its 65-horsepower motor. It was covered mostly with fabric, not metal. It had no electrical system and no radio. This meant it had no electrical starter—you started it by heading it into the wind, chocking the wheels, setting the brakes and hand throttle, switching the magneto on, and yanking the propeller through by hand. It sat nose high on its two front wheels, tail on the ground. The flying fraternity calls its kind a 'rag-wing tail dragger,' a term of endearment.

This sweet little plane, a 1946 Taylorcraft BC12D, was quite a find, partly because its seller agreed to let me keep it in its accustomed home at the Bedford airport. The hangar rent was only $25/month. It would mean a 35-mile drive from Bloomington, but I could see no alternative anyway. The Bloomington airport had a waiting list for hangars several months long, and a rental rate about six times as high as Bedford's. And to fly in and out of Bedford with no radio was relatively easy, because Bedford was a quiet airport with no control tower, Bloomington a busy one with a control tower.

None of this provoked any public comment until Tomi became mayor. About four months after the 1983 election, I picked up the paper and saw myself the subject of a headline: "Hot Line. Mr. Allison keeps airplane in Bedford." An anonymous investigative reporter had discovered my secret.

Jim starts "The Family Airplane" (photo undated, uncredited)

QUESTION—The other day a friend told me that Mayor Tomi Allison's husband keeps an airplane at the Bedford airport instead of the Bloomington (Monroe County) airport because it is a few dollars cheaper. I understand they use the excuse that the airplane doesn't have radios, but I'm also told that a lot of airplanes operate at the Monroe County Airport without radios. Mayor Allison has recently done a lot of complaining about people spending money in other communities—moving the I.U. football game to Indianapolis, for example. I wonder how she justifies keeping the family airplane in Bedford? L. W., Bloomington. (Note: 'L. W., Bloomington' turned out to be a *Herald-Telephone* staffer. I learned her identity almost immediately, but kept mum and remain so.)

ANSWER—Bloomington Mayor Tomi Allison said there were several reasons . . . (Tomi in her answer mentioned the waiting list and my preference for smaller airports and grass airstrips, and said the comparison was false.) Tom Boone, manager of the Monroe County Airport, told HOT LINE that hangar space at the airport was now available. Mayor Allison said if Boone wished, he could contact her husband and try to get him to rent a hangar in Bloomington.

Mayor Allison tries to milk a goat. (Photo by Eugene H. Ammon, June 21, 1986.)

I recall no such contact, and stayed in Bedford.

The other HOT LINE inquiries that day dealt with celebrity actress Brooke Shields, quilted windows, a missing phone number, emergency fuel service, and a late-night phone call from a credit card company. The one about me headed the list."[3]

 C380C380C380

MILE 8

In the fall of 1987, my eighth election, the Republicans smelled blood. They had not held the mayor's office for sixteen years. They thought they had a strong ticket, and saw the Democrats divided. The *Herald-Telephone* had endorsed me before, but this time endorsed my opponent. Republican realtor Tim Ellis easily raised more campaign money than I, $71,000 to $56,000, as I found out some years later.[4]

The primary had certainly revealed Democratic division. Moreover, the fall ballot had two candidates likely to draw more votes from me than from Ellis: Al Towell, running as an Independent Democrat, and Mike Andrews, running on a Grass Roots ticket.

Unlike Jack Morrison, my previous mayoral opponent, Ellis had strong financial and political backing from the Republican Party. His campaign staged a media blitz. There were full-page newspaper ads: Tim Ellis posing with Governor Robert Orr, Ellis posing with Lieutenant Governor John Mutz. The blitz notwithstanding, Republican Mayor Bob Stewart, of Columbus, Indiana, felt it necessary to warn Ellis about my service as a ribbon cutter. "She goes to all of those openings," he said. "If you open your refrigerator door, she's there! She's going to be hard to beat."

The *Herald-Telephone* sniped away. One editorial criticized me for taking too much credit for downtown redevelopment; everyone knew that the real mover and shaker was Cook CFC.

It was high school all over again.

The most substantial issue was the PCB cleanup, a seemingly endless source of hostile newspaper coverage. On this point Ellis' attacks were relatively mild. He thought the city should hire a full-time scientist to oversee the PCB cleanup. We replied that the city already had a local PCB project coordinator in John Langley, of the city utilities department, plus an experienced firm in Princeton, New Jersey, for scientific and technical work on the cleanup.[5]

Al Towell was usually less temperate. He charged that the city could not keep Westinghouse from building an unsafe PCB incinerator unless the city went to court to change the Consent Decree. He called my actions under the Consent Decree " . . . entirely futile and without effect (and) local control . . . a joke." My administration of the Consent Decree was "incompetent," and my promises to study alternatives were mere "public relations."[6]

Mike Andrews attacked both me and the structure of government. Our seven-member city Utilities Board was the city's legal representative in the PCB cleanup under the court-enforced Consent Decree. Andrews called the board the mayor's political tool to retain control of the cleanup. (Four members were appointed by the mayor, three by the city council.) Andrews wanted a referendum to transfer control to the city council. He had about three weeks to collect the 1,400 signatures needed to put the measure on the fall ballot.[7]

In other news Ellis urged me to appoint a committee to search for a new police chief—he alleged a Bloomington crime wave and low police morale—and challenged me to a one-on-one debate in addition to the pubic forum already scheduled, where all four candidates would appear. Towell charged that city drinking water was not tested properly; the city utilities director dismissed the charge. Towell vowed to improve the status of women in the city; I pointed out the number of women who already served as city department heads. I also thought of the long, patient search required in our successful quest to hire Bloomington's first woman fire fighter.

So it went, seemingly all year long.

Liz Brown, an I.U. student, mused about my "tough times." "At times, Allison has been accused of everything from insensitivity to residents' views to selling out the city to Westinghouse and setting it adrift in a cesspool of hazardous waste. She's been heckled at public meetings and harassed in print. And she wants the job for another four years." I explained that another victory would preserve my winning team of city hall department heads and employees, who had been such fun to watch in their conscientious work for the city.[8]

Congressmen Lee Hamilton and Frank McCloskey (the former mayor) endorsed me in early October. Later that month a poll conducted by the *Herald-Telephone* showed me with a wide lead over Ellis, and wider leads over Towell and Andrews. However, many voters, about 30%, were "undecided." The same poll revealed the PCB cleanup as the big issue among voters.

The four-way forum went about the way I expected. My three opponents concentrated on the cleanup, traffic planning, and police management. I tried to frame the crossfire as distorted attacks that portrayed our community as worse than residents knew it to be.[9]

It was no landslide, but I won with 261 more votes than Ellis. It was only a plurality, 44.3% to 42.1% (5,155-4,894), but it was enough. The other two candidates drew 13.6%. Andrews had 7.6% (884), and Towell 6.0% (694). On the city council the 6-3 Democratic majority slipped to 5-4. According to the *Herald-Telephone*, some thought Andrews and Towell had cut into my vote, and others thought they had cut Ellis' vote. I think it likely that many "undecided" voters went for Ellis on election day.[10]

According to the paper's opinion page, the vote revealed

widespread concern about City Hall. The paper pointed out that I had received 2,200 fewer votes than in 1983. It conceded my reelection, but saw an obvious loss of confidence in the city administration, i.e., me.[11]

My own opinion was that the steady media barrage of scary PCB stories would have hurt any mayor's chance of reelection.

In a letter to the editor a student took issue with the paper. "I am only a junior in high school, but I find the field of politics very intriguing. I have trouble understanding why the *Herald-Telephone*'s editorials are so unjustly spiteful towards Tomi Allison. How can you call an election victory a 'stinging rebuke from city voters'? This female candidate beat three male opponents. True, she received less than 50 percent of the votes. But, considering that there are four candidates altogether, 44 percent is a pretty decent margin. Some of our greatest presidents such as Truman and Kennedy were elected with less than 50 percent of the vote. Yet, nobody considered these men's elections a loss. Rebecca Demetrius."[12]

Tim Ellis' campaign mantra had proclaimed "It's Time"— meaning time for a change. Jim thought the Republicans could recycle Tim's yard signs in the next election cycle by means of a minor edit: Insert "Still" between "It's" and "Time."

CHAPTER 10

Pleasantries

COMMUNITY FOUNDATION OF BLOOMINGTON AND MONROE COUNTY: BIRTH PANGS

Following is the text of a speech I gave at a Community Foundation celebration on February 10, 2009. The foundation now holds about $22 million in assets, and has awarded over $15 million in grants.

ᙅᔓᔔᙂ

What makes a community attractive? Prosperity; culture; arts; education; recreation; all in beautiful surroundings. Most newcomers praise all of those, but what they like most is that "Welcome to Bloomington!" feeling. We truly welcome their participation as integral members of our community. This is not mere magic. What builds a sense of community is people working together in a common cause.

Bloomington was once a series of separate communities: The university, the town, the west side. When we began to work together we became the Bloomington community. Today we celebrate a vital part of that tapestry, the Community Foundation of Bloomington and Monroe County.

A telling example of its work is its Matchstick Program, where the foundation matches one third of our contributions to selected organizations. By targeting these organizations this way, the foundation both highlights their merits and encourages others to give. The Matchstick Program can give the decisive boost an organi-

I.U. Chancellor Herman B Wells, September 18, 1986 (uncredited photo, autographed)

zation may need to reach its critical mass. In its first three years Matchstick generated $450,000.

How did it all start?

In 1988 I had been mayor for five years. To meet great public demand for new social services, we had used as much federal money as we could. We had added local tax moneys. But we never had enough money to meet public demand. Our community needed new resources.

Columbus caught my envious eye. That city, although smaller than ours, had no less than three foundations, all established by J. Irwin Miller of Cummins Engines. And what a boon those foundations had been. They had put Columbus on the map as a world center of modern architecture. Why couldn't Bloomington have a community foundation for a variety of needs: social, cultural, educational and recreational?

My staff approved the idea of a community foundation, but then they were always gung ho. When I tried it out around town, it had a cold reception. "We already have the I.U. Foundation. We already have the Hospital Foundation. We already have United Way. Isn't that enough? Wouldn't a new community foundation compete for scarce community resources?" There were many discouraging words.

It was time to visit our great wise man, the respected sage of both town and gown, Herman B Wells. He agreed that Bloomington needed a community foundation. Such a foundation would encourage more giving. He said I would need help in getting started. He said the university should provide help. In fact, through his advocacy the university did provide our nascent foundation with a dollar-a-year man from the Business School, Jack Mulholland, whose skills proved invaluable. Jack and his wife led by example: One of the foundation's endowed funds bears their names.

In my State of the City Address in 1988 I announced our intent to start a community foundation, and the newspaper headlined the announcement. Now on record, we had to come through.

This difficult task went to Sue Wheeler, our Director of Human Resources. For expert guidance we went to the national network of foundations, which provided materials and advice. CFC gave office space in Fountain Square. Every year, for several years, from my Mayor's Office Budget I gave $17,000 for foundation staff. We called it progress, but outside City Hall community leaders still failed to see the value of a community foundation. We needed to show that our foundation was to be more than some parasitical creature of City Hall. We needed a citizen-advocate to breathe new life into the foundation.

As luck would have it, the perfect advocate soon appeared like a genie in a bottle. Ilknur Ralston walked into my office and declared herself a volunteer: She wanted to work for something meaningful for the community. I could scarcely believe my ears. There was this energetic, vivacious, capable young lady, an experienced organizer, a professional accountant, married to another one, Bob Ralston, who would also befriend the foundation. I explained the vision, and she embraced it. She accepted the job, knowing full well how difficult the task would be, and set to work immediately. Two years later, in 1990, the new foundation was incorporated. Its first Director was Kathleen Wissing. Ilknur gave it her full attention for many years to come, and finally saw it take hold and grow strong.

This foundation owes so much of its success to community donors and volunteers. It also owes much to the Lilly Foundation for seminars and matching funds that gave a decisive boost when it counted. How right it then seems that our foundation's Matchstick Program stands ready and able to give local organizations their own decisive boost at the opportune time.

People helping people. That is what builds a community, and that is the story of the foundation we celebrate today.

CB80

PAUL NEWMAN!

I never met Paul Newman, but one of his biggest fans, who also never met him, came into my life through our Sister City Program.

Sharon Hall, a sassy intense Taiwanese, was self-appointed mother to many Asian newcomers scattered across the city and campus. Wife of an American engineer who had met her in Taiwan, she was the biological mother of two teen-age boys. She herself had never accepted the role of dutiful Chinese daughter, but expected her boys to be dutiful Chinese-American sons.

Her attitude toward me was respectful, but left no doubt of her determination to forge an official Sister City relation between Bloomington and some community in Taiwan or even mainland China. Committees were formed. Letters were exchanged. Diplomats were approached. Personal contacts were exploited. At last it all fell into place: A delegation of Bloomingtonians fastened their seat belts and took off for Taiwan, bearing gifts of local artifacts that included a basketball autographed by Bobby Knight, the celebrity coach of I.U. basketball. On the long flight west Sharon Hall had plenty of time to coach us in the Chinese for "thank you" and other handy expressions.

Distant memory tells me that our jet-lagged group went straight from the airport to an elaborate lunch hosted by the mayor of Luchow, the candidate sister city. Painted red and gold, the restaurant sparkled with ladies in elegant cheongsams with slit skirts and mandarin collars. Sharon identified and translated the dishes, of which I recall only deep-fried baby octopi—exotic but tasty—and steamed sea urchins, merely exotic. The mayor stood and offered a toast. Jim said I should offer a toast; I stood and said a few words that were translated and well received.

As a female mayor I was a curiosity wherever I traveled in Asia, but always treated with kindness and deference. Sharon translated approving comments from the crowd: "She looks like a mayor." In a crowded restaurant a little girl approached our table and said something to Sharon. "She wants to touch your hair." My white hair was a rarity in Taiwan. I was pleased to oblige.

Mercedes limos hurried us off to our hotel in a melee of Japanese cars and smoking two-stroke motor scooters. The crushing density of the pedestrian traffic soon seemed almost normal. So did our breakfast fare of stewed salty plums, pot stickers, watery rice and peanuts.

The following days were a blur of rain, heat, temples, ingenious jade carvings, cheering school children, tour buses, racing pigeons, Sun Moon Lake, jump rope teams, Taroko Gorge, aboriginal dancers, I.U. alumni and frog lips soup. On a remote seacoast we found a pair of American Mormon missionaries like two notes washed ashore in a bottle.

We shivered through dinner in a high mountain inn that had little heat or hot water; our serving waiters wore down-lined vests and fingerless gloves. The next day our traveling companions kidded about finding a dog to eat, in the belief that one can keep warm by eating dog meat. According to the local joke, "There are no old dogs in Taiwan."

One night in Taipei Sharon took us through Snake Alley, a shadowy haunt of pickpockets and prostitutes. There was a vigorous market for venomous snakes, whose fresh blood was prized as an aphrodisiac. One merchant proved the fighting spirit of his cobra by pairing it with a mongoose. Sharon wanted us to try a street vendor's roasted pigeon on a stick, but we were not hungry. Neither was she.

CRITOCRITO

Jim impressed the ladies in the Luchow mayor's entourage. As he tells it: "I was presentable, but utterly lacking in movie glamour. Still, I could see how someone not accustomed to Americans, given a chance to see them up close, might see more than was really there. That's what happened to me, with a little help from Sharon Hall. One afternoon, after a few toasts, I could see Sharon and the ladies putting their heads together, with me as the subject of their conference. When they broke their huddle, Sharon had it down: 'Paul Newman! He looks like Paul Newman!' And it stuck, but only when Sharon was there to ladle on the glue."

⋄

After we returned to Bloomington, Luchow became our Sister City, and the two cities had a few cultural exchanges. Sharon arranged another official trip to Taiwan, and one to mainland China. She saw to it that I was a regular celebrant of Chinese New Year in Bloomington, and we continued our friendship after I left office.

⋄⋄

She and Jim took a motorcycle ride together. Jim said, "Toward the end of her life Sharon struggled with a number of illnesses. One day I happened to be alone when she phoned from a doctor's office. She needed a ride home; could I help her? I explained that Tomi was gone with our car; all I had was a motorcycle. After a couple of beats she said that would be o.k.; when could I get there? I stuck my spare helmet on the Harley's sissy bar and found her waiting in the doctor's parking lot. I helped her fasten the helmet, steadied the bike as she climbed on and took it slow and easy on the way to her house. Nevertheless, her helmet banged into mine at every stop sign. She enjoyed the ride; it reminded her of happy girlhood days in Taiwan, a rebellious free spirit aboard her motor scooter.

The last time I saw her she took a while to answer the front door. When it finally opened there she stood, with her usual, 'Aaaah! Paul Newman!'"

⋄

THE BEAST OF BRYAN PARK

". . . terrestrial carnivores of moderate size distinguished by a curious crest or dorsal sail supported by greatly elongated neural spines of the vertebrae . . . ." Description from *Webster's Third New International Dictionary.*

Our house is a few blocks northeast of Bryan Park, a favorite place for morning and evening walks. Its playgrounds are a magnet for children. One of those playgrounds is home to a unique structure children find irresistible. It somehow beckons them to climb, crawl or sit all over its scaly hide. It might be a dinosaur, it might be a dragon. Nearly ten feet long, it is almost four feet high at its highest point, and three feet wide at its widest. Its tail loops up and around, tipped with four warlike spikes draped across the thing's right rear side. Its head, turned about twenty degrees to its right, wears a crocodilian smirk. This much is certain. It is a massive, elaborate limestone carving. It has endured at least one playground remodeling, and seems unlikely to change location any time soon. It is not standard playground fare. How did it get there?

When fresh visitors come to our Elm Heights neighborhood, we like to walk them past the abundant traces of art left by generations of limestone carvers—ornate bird baths, sun dials, benches, friezes, lintels, pilasters, and smiling lions recumbent. We happen to live in a neighborhood where it was once commonplace to pretty one's house with this kind of art. Much of it was done by home-owning carvers who made good livings in the heyday of the limestone industry. With its decline such carvings grew scarce, but still appear occasionally on new public buildings. A prominent example is the Yankee Stadium that opened in 2009. Much of that, and of many other iconic buildings in Manhattan and Washington, D.C., came from limestone quarries near Bloomington.

An especially ornate example is Simon Hall, a science building that opened in 2007 on the campus of Indiana University, Bloomington. The entrance to its Gill Conference Center has archways with limestone carvings, in extraordinary detail, of a series of creatures called "The Chemistry of Life": RNA, E. coli, Paramecium, maize, mice and fruit flies. In collaboration with faculty members, sculptor Amy Brier created these remarkable figures in clay. They were then rendered in limestone by artisan carvers of Indiana Limestone Co. Inc. Some older buildings on campus display the carver's art in a whimsical vein, a smattering of limestone gargoyles.

The city's Arts Commission wanted to highlight limestone carving and asked the city to sponsor a contest. I suggested carved limestone benches destined for our public parks. I announced the proposal in May, 1989, as the Hoosierfest Limestone Bench Carving Contest. Local stone carvers could submit their entries by the end of the month, and winning benches would be placed in parks around town.

Artists were asked to submit a drawing or model, and indicate dimensions and any relevant features. Entries would be judged by a committee of experts: a Fine Arts faculty member from Indiana University, and one representative each from Bloomington's Department of Parks and Recreation, and Bedford's Limestone Institute. They would judge the designs in terms of function, aesthetics, and comfort. Each finalist would be assigned to a stone company that would furnish free stone.

Contest spokesperson Rebecca Stover expected contestants to range from professional stone carvers to community artists. She expected a variety of styles and means, from hand tools to air compressors. First, second, and third prizes would be $900, $700, and $500. Contest cosponsors were the Bloomington Arts Commission, Bloomington Parks and Recreation, Hoosierfest '89, and the Limestone Institute. Winners would be announced at the Hoosierfest in September.[1]

Come September, the winner emerged: the Dimetrodon dinosaur by William Galloway, a resident of Brown County and a stone carver for Bybee Stone Co., which donated the stone. Galloway had spent six weeks and 180 hours making his bench.

His first thought was a Stegosaurus, which he rejected as too uncomfortable for a bench. The sail-backed Dimetrodon was a better choice, especially when he improved on nature by adding a Stegosaurus tail to his four-ton creature. He had tried for realism and versatility. The body and feet had the right shape. "You sit on the legs and the back and the head and you can climb

Tomi and the Dimetrodon, 2005. Photo by James Allison.

through the tail, which loops around. I made it as a sculpture you could sit on or play on." At the judging site playful children soon put it to the test. The artist laughed: "There are lots of little footprints all over it. They won't hurt it." And its time in Bryan Park has proven him right.

Galloway won second prize too, for a bench that evoked opposing wings. It went to People's Park on Kirkwood. Third prize went to David Rodgers of Bloomington, for a "fulcrum" bench that went to a wooded area of Bryan Park. Additional prizes went to Pennie Baxter, Bedford, for an "interlocking" bench that went to the Ballinger Art Center in Cascades Park, and Basil Wampler, Bloomington, for a "traditional carved bench." Other donor quarries were Hoadley, Fluck Stone, Independent Limestone, Reed, and Woolery Mill.

Rosemary Fraser, a member of the Bloomington Arts Commission, thought the contest was a great way to impress the community with its limestone heritage. "We thought that for a first try, it was tremendously successful and we would be excited about trying it again. The art that came out of it was all great."[2]

Alas, it was not to be a recurring event. The 1989 competition remains our first and only limestone bench contest. Everything Rosemary Fraser said was true. Unfortunately, as she may have known better than anyone else, like so many other good things it was a great deal harder to bring off than it looked. A more durable celebration, the Indiana Limestone Sculpture Symposium, began in 1996 and takes place annually near the Bybee Stone Co. in Ellettsville. There the public can interact with limestone artists from all over the world.

LADY OF MAINE: MARGARET CHASE SMITH, DECEMBER 14, 1897–MAY 29, 1995

When we heard that Margaret Chase Smith had died of a stroke at age 97, my husband and I recalled a dinner party with Herman B Wells, the legendary Chancellor of Indiana University, at his home on Tenth Street. The occasion, around commencement day in May 1989, was a visit to Bloomington by Herman's old friend from Maine, the first woman elected to the U.S. Senate. At dinner I sat across from her; Jim sat between her and her traveling companion, who had been a high-ranking military nurse. The two other guests, I.U. President Tom Ehrlich and his wife, Ellen, soon left for a commencement engagement.

Senator Smith's conversation was memorable. Jim asked about the Russians she had known. As she talked of her interactions with Molotov, Stalin's Foreign Minister, it occurred to him that his meeting with her had connected him through a chain of handshakes with Roosevelt, Churchill, Stalin and Lenin. Also in the chain was Senator Joe McCarthy, with whom she accidentally shared the Congressional tram as she rode to make her famous speech on the floor of the Senate, the first public denunciation of the great Red Baiter by a major politician, a member of his own party.

Jim told of our first visit to Washington. A friend, who worked for a Senator, showed us the Senate parking garage. The car Jim remembered was Senator Smith's 1946 Plymouth coupe–a dusty gray eminence, then more than a quarter century old, figured against a background of shiny new cars. She remembered it fondly. It had a stick shift.

She questioned Jim, an experimental psychologist, about his work. He told her about his animal model for the study of economics. She wanted to know how one could learn about economics from experiments on rats, and he explained behavioral prices and wage rates. Their conversation turned to his hobby, sport aviation. She wanted to know how gliders could fly so far, and he talked of thermals and glide ratios.

He mentioned our first glimpse of Maine, in the summer of 1986, when we drove down from Quebec City and rounded a bend in the woods to behold a shimmering sunlit lake right off a picture postcard. She named the lake, and invited us to visit her in Skowhegan.

We never managed to do that, but we hope to visit her library there.

CHAPTER 11

The Campaign Trail, Miles 9 and 10

MILE 9

My ninth election was relatively quiet. Although PCBs were still a political issue, the Growth Policy Plan held center stage in the Republican opposition. This time I had three opponents in the primary, and the personalities displayed a wide spectrum of local color.[1]

Ronald Crose, a self-styled "labor journalist," promised to appoint fifteen women and five men as department heads, poor people who understood Bloomington as it truly was. I thought that had its merits, but Crose spent much of the campaign season in jail, distracted by various charges involving alcohol abuse, resistance to arrest, and harassment. He received 54 votes in the May 7 primary.

F. D. R. Enochs, a retired utilities department employee, ran as the candidate of working people and senior citizens who would actually do something about PCBs, not just talk. That sounded good, but he received only 62 votes.

Natasha Jacobs was an I.U. graduate student. I liked what she wanted, but I was already doing it: safer streets for children to walk to school; infrastructure improvements; improvement of core neighborhoods and the downtown; affordable housing; well-paid jobs; high-quality industry; stronger enforcement of parking codes; bike paths. She garnered 366 votes.

I focused on my desire to continue the city's progress in environmental preservation, downtown revitalization, economic health, planning of future growth, street improvement, and the City Hall/ Showers project. Maybe the voters liked what we had done, and thought we would do more of the same. My vote total was 1,631.

Running for mayor on the Republican side, but perhaps more PATI—People Against the Incinerator—than Republican, was County Clerk Jim Fielder. He collected 753 votes. He planned to step up his anti-incinerator efforts, and expected the voters to come through: "I predict that the mayor will be trying to pull a magic rabbit out of her hat to save this election. But I think the people are wise to this and won't let it happen."

He went on to blame me for the delay in the Walnut Street utility project, which ran over a month past its scheduled completion date. I said it would be finished by the end of the week. I added that the delays were the fault of private contractors not controlled by the city.[2]

MILE 10

My final election would come in November, 1991. Long before we got there, the Republican side began to fall apart.

In late June Jim Fielder withdrew. He cited medical problems connected with a history of reconstructive hip surgery. He mentioned insufficient support from the Republican party, and alluded to disorganization and a lack of leadership. He may have had additional reasons.

Fielder regretted the disappointment to his supporters, but had encouraging words for his replacement. "I do not want to see Tomi go unchallenged. I think she is very vulnerable this year, and has waffled on too many issues. We have had nine years of the Allison administration and it's been too much." The Republican county chairman, Steve Hogan, promised a timely replacement.

The Coalition Opposed to PCB Ash in Monroe County (COPA) regretted Fielder's departure. (Residents formed COPA when they thought their upscale property might be a likely site for the disposal of ashes incidental to incineration.) COPA President Mike Baker supported Fielder's anti-incinerator stand. Baker said, "He brought interesting discussions to the race concerning the whole consent decree and PCB cleanup. We are still supportive of any candidate, regardless of party, who will work to help clean up PCB contamination without incineration."[3]

Several weeks later, in August, Belint Vazsonyi (pronounced "Vahzhnee") stepped forward as the replacement Republican candidate for mayor. A Hungarian-born concert pianist on the I.U. School of Music faculty, he was a recent resident with scant name recognition. He had no direct experience in local politics, and had never voted in Bloomington. Nevertheless, COPA immediately embraced his anti-incinerator stance.

The third candidate was Ron Smith, of the Independent Voters Party. Smith, a technician employed in the water testing lab of the city utilities department, focused on criticism of the PCB cleanup. His campaign often annoyed John Langley, the city's project coordinator for the cleanup. For example, one of Smith's ads showed rocks that were supposedly required by the Consent Decree to be burned in the proposed incinerator. In fact, they were to be decontaminated, put back in place, and capped. Another showed Smith standing before a pile of ugly scrap metal that he said was to be incinerated. Actually, the metal had already been decontaminated and would soon be sold as scrap.[4]

What follows are my impressions of the campaign, based on personal notes. Vazsonyi began to inform himself by touring various city departments, such as police and utilities, under the guidance of city department heads. In the press he slammed me for unproductive expenditures on the PCB cleanup. (A *Herald-Times* reporter wanted to know how much it had cost for my trip to Tucson to examine a possible alternative to incineration.) Vazsonyi promised, but later denied, that he would abolish any master plan for development.

The paper, noting how often my Deputy Mayor, Mike Davis, responded to Vazsonyi's criticisms, wanted to know who was mayor, Tomi Allison or Mike Davis?

A poll showed that my campaign was in good shape.

The League of Women Voters debate in City Council Chambers had standing room only. Ron Smith made sure I had plenty of PCB hecklers in the crowd. I zapped Vazsonyi for dissing city workers. I was pleased with the debate.

Mick Harrison, the leader of INPIRG (Indiana Public Interest Research Group), tried to subpoena me to testify about the cleanup. Jeff Grodner, the city's PCB attorney, had the subpoena quashed, as Harrison had no legal standing in the matter.

We were running short of campaign funds, and needed money for radio spots. We had to curtail our newspaper ads. Matt Pierce, a staffer at the Indiana State House, gave me frequent campaign advice. It usually ended with "Don't lose your cool." As usual, I was doing a lot of walking and conversing in the neighborhoods, a campaign custom with which I felt comfortable.

In the meantime we worked like beavers on crucial city business: the master plan; the geographic information system; a community health clinic that never quite materialized. At a press conference Vazsonyi asked for a two-month delay in cleanup permits; the Indiana Department of Environmental Management denied his request. The campus yawned and woke up; the I.U. Student Association asked for a meeting and a debate.

On the up side, I spoke at a Rotary Club meeting, where Republicans came forward and quietly offered financial and other support. On the down side, two Democratic candidates for City Council asked for a statewide referendum on incineration.

Rumor declared a big disagreement between Vazsonyi and the publisher of the *Herald-Times*. In any event, the paper endorsed no candidate for mayor, Republican or otherwise.

A real estate developer rented a room where he staged a fund-raiser for Vazsonyi and offered to give one dollar for every dollar raised by his fellow developers.

I appeared at a meeting of AFSCME (American Federation of State, County, and Municipal Employees), a union with which I had long enjoyed good relations. I thought the hostile reception undeserved. After the meeting I was told that Ron Smith had been working on some of the union members. I had good receptions at two Kiwanis clubs, the Downtown and the Golden Age.

Vazsonyi complained: Why was I so angry at him?

Music Professor Harvey Phillips staged a fund raiser for me, with excellent results. One of Vazsonyi's musical colleagues slammed me in a letter to the editor for attending concerts only during election years. Some of Vazsonyi's musical colleagues began to appoach me with offers of support for my campaign.

I got a kick out of the Older Americans Center, where I had a favorable reception at its 20-year celebration. Vazsonyi attended uninvited. Later in the celebration, at a meet-the-candidates function on the second floor, nobody came to meet the candidates: All of these older Americans had better things to do down on the first floor.

We opened Third Street Park on October 26. At the opening ceremony some weighty Republicans promised me their personal votes and financial support.

At a news conference I reported that 83% of Vazsonyi's support came from four developers. As it turned out, he spent about twice as much as I, $71,036 to $35,430.[5]

A Rotary club sponsored a debate at the Poplars on the I.U. campus and the university station, WTIU, televised a one-hour call-in show. I thought both went well. Matt Pierce repeated his admonition, "Don't lose your cool." More money came in.

At a news conference I disclosed that Vazsonyi had never voted, and I repeated his dependence on developers.

Four days before the election, Channel 6 TV came down from Indianapolis. What were the major issues? Vazsonyi said "PCBs." I said "No. The master plan."

It was good to win big in a three-way race that seemed to mark Bloomington as a multiparty town of Democrats, Republicans, and Independents: Allison 4,856 (50.6%), Vazsonyi 2,886 (30%), and Smith 1,864 (19.4%). In addition, Democrats did well in city council races, rising from 5-4 to an 8-1 majority.

I called the election a vote of confidence in my administration's achievements, and a mandate for our new Growth Policy Plan (the "master plan"). Vazsonyi made some gracious remarks about the outcome. Smith fired some parting shots with a promise "to prosecute the Allison administration for their criminal offenses."

I thought the campaign was marred by petty personal comments that antagonized some voters. It also revealed my monetary value: "It showed that at least a couple of people are willing to put down $10,000 to see me defeated." Truly, many of Vazsonyi's big supporters were developers and builders hot to derail the master plan.

Again Vazsonyi portrayed the incinerator as a threat to the environment. I replied that the voters had seen through the scare tactics and recognized the Consent Decree as the best protection for the community. That was more than I could say of my state legislator and my congressman, both prominent Democrats. One had called for an opening of the Consent Decree. The other had introduced federal legislation to outlaw trash-fueled incineration.

I rejected the role of lame duck mayor. I would announce re-election intentions when the time came. As goals I mentioned the downtown convention center, street construction projects, and the project at the old Showers furniture building: the research park, the office complex, and the new City Hall.[6]

Belint Vazsonyi took no further part in local politics. Years later, in Washington, D.C., he resurfaced in a right-wing think tank. Interviewed on C-Span television, he reminisced briefly about his run for mayor. It was a good experience, he said, but he never expected to win. How could he win against a popular female mayor who had held office for years?

Mayor Allison with Los Angeles Mayor Tom Bradley, in Bloomington to celebrate the 1911 founding, at I.U., of black fraternity Kappa Alpha Psi. (Photo uncredited and undated, but probably 1991.)

GRANDMA BLOOMINGTON

If it had been up to the newspaper, few Bloomingtonians would have known me on sight. The paper explained the near blackout in terms of its policy not to publish photos of the mayor at ribbon cutting ceremonies. Never mind that my motive for such appearances was not political, but to boost fledgling businesses.

It was television that brought me widespread recognition in the community, and made strangers feel they could approach me. Some Bloomingtonians kept an eye on city government by tuning to a local-access TV channel that broadcast city council meetings. Viewers would often see me as I addressed the council about various issues of particular concern to the Mayor's Office. On the same channel they might see me as the host of a do-it-yourself show called "Your City at Work," in which I interviewed various department heads who explained their work and the services their departments provided.

I had asked our university radio station, WFIU, to provide a similar program about city departments and services. The flat refusal was based on the lofty notion that WFIU was a regional station, not a local one. At last, many years later, the station began to broadcast a weekly show about the mayor's office in Bloomington and other nearby cities.

But back in the day, frequent exposure on local access TV could make my face familiar to its viewing audience, children as well as adults. A stranger stopped me in the grocery store, as strangers often did. "Mayor Allison, I have to tell you something about my four-year-old daughter." In the store a few weeks earlier she had caught sight of me in the course of their grocery shopping. Excitedly she tugged at his sleeve. "Look, Daddy! It's Grandma Bloomington!"

It was that white hair again.

GIFT TO A CONSTITUENT

Like many university towns, Bloomington stood at the forefront of the conservation movement. During my administration we set up a recycling center, hired a director, and distributed red plastic bins to households throughout the city. Citizens who wanted to recycle could fill the bins and put them out for special city crews, who would dump the contents into their trucks and leave the empty bins at the curb.

One evening my husband and I drove to an old stone farm house for dinner with an honorary social club, The Kentucky Colonels. As the evening progressed and the diners relaxed our hostess announced she had a story for the mayor. On a visit to her aged mother at a nursing home their conversation had somehow turned to local politicians. To her surprise, her mother had definite ideas about the lot of them. "I'm all for that nice Mayor Allison," she said, "and that's a fact."

"But why, Mother?"

"Because she's the only one who ever gave me anything."

"She gave you something? What did she give you?"

"Come on, I'll show you."

The mother led the way into the bathroom, switched on the light and pointed at a plastic container. "There," she said proudly. "She gave me that red clothes hamper!"

Of course it was one of those red recycling bins from the city. But if Mother thought it a personal gift from the mayor, that was fine with Daughter.

A TALE OF FOUR CITIES

I know four midwestern Bloomingtons, in four different states: Indiana, Illinois, Wisconsin, and Minnesota. A confusion among them once caused the temporary disappearance of an entire German band, and a red-light-running bus ride through our town.

It all started when a local organization invited the band from a small German town to perform in Bloomington. The band landed at Chicago O'Hare and boarded a bus for the trip to Indiana. However, the American bus driver insisted on taking his bus load of musicians to Bloomington, Illinois. The Germans protested, but none spoke English very well and the driver, who spoke no German, prevailed. In a few hours, as we wondered where they were, they arrived at our Illinois namesake, where nobody knew what to do with them. Eventually we got a phone call from an Illinois official, who sent them on their way to Indiana.

When their bus pulled in we gave them an interpreter, and asked how we could compensate for their inconvenience. Was there anything the city could do for them? The interpreter came back: Yes, there was. Maybe it was too much to ask, but—could it be possible? Could a police car escort their bus through the streets of Bloomington, straight through several red lights, siren full blast, with side traffic halted as their bus flew through the intersections?

I knew this kind of fantasy. When people told me what they liked best about the prospect of being mayor, they would often mention such things as a citywide privilege to park where one pleased, impervious to meter maids (I never had that), or a private parking space at City Hall (I never accepted mine).

I thought the band deserved to be humored. I phoned the police chief, who agreed. He devised a route on the outskirts of town where the requested escort would not disrupt traffic too much. The Germans and I climbed aboard the bus, and our little procession started to roll. Each time we ran a red light the passengers let out a big cheer.

In return, we enjoyed a wonderful public concert in the town square in front of the county courthouse. There's nothing like a German band.

IN BRIEF

One of the greatest privileges of being mayor was the chance to see so many American subcultures. A memorable example arose with an invitation from the Reserve Officers Training Corps at Indiana University. Would the mayor attend the ROTC graduation ceremony?

When I accepted the invitation I was told that someone from the Corps would come to my office to give me a briefing. It seemed odd that such a simple occasion would require a briefing; I was not expected to say or do anything at the ceremony, but merely to play my customary role of a distinguished but passive member of the audience. Still, as I did not quite know what a military briefing was, I was willing to presume that the Corps knew best if it thought I needed one.

On the appointed day two young men in uniform marched into my office, a superior and a subordinate. The subordinate set up a big easel, loaded with flip charts, right in front of my desk. The superior used a pointer to indicate the highlights of each chart; when those were exhausted the subordinate flipped the chart to reveal the next one with the next set of highlights. It was amazing how many charts it took to cover such a simple occasion. Could it be an elaborate joke on an outsider?

No. The long briefing covered every detail, far beyond what I needed to know—that being the time and place of the ceremony, and where to sit. But I could see it as good practice for two young men in the ways of a proper briefing. For me it was a peek at another American subculture. And I seldom refused such requests as theirs, because I saw them as opportunities to fulfill the ceremonial role of the mayor's office, a role of great importance to the community.

CHAPTER 12

Downtown

When you're alone, and life is making you lonely
You can always go
Downtown

~ Petula Clark

Well, Petula, not always.

In 1963, when I first saw it, downtown Bloomington was not much of a pick-me-up. In the 1970s Mayor Frank McCloskey and businessman Dick Schmaltz became historic downtown boosters when they led the drive to build a parking garage next to the Graham Hotel. There was talk of putting government offices into the Graham, but it was only talk. The great surge of downtown development began in the 1980s and continues to this day, but always in the face of opposing forces that would smash the vital nucleus of the city.

In the 1960s, shopping malls and big-box retail stores began to decimate the businesses that had thrived downtown for decades. In Bloomington store closings left empty fronts all around the square. Businesses on Kirkwood, the street that connects the square with the I.U. campus on the east, did better than those on the square. Mayor McCloskey had invested in Kirkwood, but the efficacy of his famous Kirkwood planters was controversial.

They looked nice, but their streetward projection narrowed the roadway and shortened the turn radii, making it all too easy for a routine right turn to put the car on top of the planter and into the body shop. Whatever good the planters may have done for business along Kirkwood, it was not enough to stop the steady flight of shoe stores, pharmacies, department and hardware stores.

Jane Jacobs' book, *The Death and Life of Great American Cities*,[1] had led me to champion the livable town. I believed in two essential elements for the vitality of any city: It had to have a center, and it had to have livable, walkable neighborhoods.

As a member of the city council I started beautification efforts with a Clean Cities campaign (our slogan was "Fight Dirty"), a Tree City program, and ordinances to improve handling of trash and litter. I talked the mayor into budgeting a half-time position for city landscaping. When I became mayor the position went to full time, and we started a street-tree replacement program throughout the city under the direction of Lee Huss. We landscaped planters around town, and paid to maintain trash cans downtown and along Kirkwood. We added a part-time employee to publicize our trash ordinances and advocate clean streets and our new recycling program.

THE NATIONAL MAIN STREET PROGRAM

About a year after I became mayor I hired Glenda Morrison (now Murray) as our Redevelopment Director, partly for her experience in the redevelopment of downtown Evansville. Off we went to a conference in Toledo on downtown revitalization, where we learned about the National Main Street Program. Under its guidance we resolved to improve our downtown economy by concentrating on three key points: downtown housing for residents, who would provide both a stable base of customers and a human presence around the clock; activities to draw people downtown; and an attractive downtown facade. When we returned from the conference I told Glenda that one of her jobs was to encourage downtown redevelopment.

The city hosted a conference on the downtown and invited business owners, neighborhood activists, and any other interested parties. Its purpose was to involve both businesses and citizens in the planning for downtown revitalization. The speakers included Fred Prall, who was developing the old Wicks Department Store, and Bill Cook, who spoke of the Graham Hotel. Cook made a big splash when he remarked that he was prepared to make a major investment in the downtown because it made economic sense.

Glenda's efforts produced a Commission for Bloomington Downtown. The commission hired Tom Gallagher as its first director, and the city paid part of his salary. Tom was followed by Talisha Coppock. The commission met regularly, at First National Bank. Glenda and I always attended; business regulars were Chuck Zebendon (First National Bank), Dick Schmaltz, Bob Snoddy (CFC Properties, a Cook Group company), Denny Moir (Ben Franklin, a small chain of arts and crafts stores), Bob Hammontree, and Bill Schrader (*Herald-Telephone*). Concerned citizens also came. Later these meetings were attended by representatives of the city departments most directly concerned with downtown businesses: Public Works, Redevelopment, Parks and Recreation, Police, and others as required. Thus, the commission came to function as a continuing interface between city government and downtown businesses. This was where business could make its problems known to government, where the two sides could develop solutions together. If you had a problem with zoning, facades, loans, lights, or parking, you took it to the commission, where it would be aired and a plan of attack formulated.

The commission also promoted events like the opening of the Fountain Square Mall on the south side of the square. It also promoted activities throughout the year, such as the Fourth of July Parade, Harvey Phillips' Tuba Santas on the square, the Easter egg hunt, the Christmas Canopy of Lights, and many others. Newspaper inserts from the commission advertised special shopping events downtown. Glenda Morrison, representing the city, and Steve Ferguson, representing CFC, told of the commission's work at speaking engagements around town and in other communities. At two nearby towns their triumphant spiel evoked an envious response: "Yeah, but you have Bill Cook!" I responded by telling them of other properties whose owners had major renovations to their credit: Wicks, Uptown, One City Center, the old jail on Walnut (turned into a bank), the old city hall (turned into Waldron Arts Center), Princess Theater, and three buildings on the south east side of the square. Many of these renovations added second-floor housing.

We had good support from the Cook interests and many downtown businesses through the Downtown Business Association. Downtown business owner Denny Moir was the most continually active and always helpful. The city provided redevelopment money for facade improvements and free design consultation. We urged downtown businesses to be more responsive to their customers. They should keep uniform hours, so that customers could combine their visits to different stores. They should recognize that parking was for the convenience of customers, not employees. We encouraged the downtown business association to meet and discuss such problems in concert.

To stimulate downtown residency, we changed the zoning laws in ways to encourage residential development on the upper floors of business buildings around the square. The new zoning allowed higher population densities than before, and specified fewer parking places for downtown developments.

We hired a St. Louis consulting firm (Peckham, Guyton and Viets) to lead our formation of a downtown plan—not an overall plan, but specific projects that would change the dynamic of downtown. Our list included the south side of the square, a new City Hall and a Convention Center—all actualized in the years that followed, if not exactly in accordance with the original plan, close enough to validate the concepts. A fourth project, housing for the elderly, still awaits development.

With the crucial support of City Councilman Lloyd Olcott, our commission would eventually spearhead the drive to make a downtown Convention Center out of a former auto agency (Tom O'Daniel Ford)—a joint project of a holding corporation, the city, the county, and the Tourism and Convention Bureau. In turn, the new Convention Center led to a new downtown hotel. The Commission for Downtown Bloomington (later called "Downtown Bloomington, Inc.") continues to promote an astonishing list of activities that draw people to the center of the city, everything from arts fairs to the Taste of Bloomington.

Downtown redevelopment attracted serious attention with Cook's first project, the restoration and remodeling of an historic landmark, the Graham Hotel. Mayor McCloskey had stimulated that project, on a handshake agreement with Bill Cook: If the city would build a parking structure next to the hotel, Cook would restore the hotel. The structure went up, and the hotel was restored.

Before the Graham restoration, a dollar invested in the downtown was widely seen as a dollar down the drain. One reason was the popular notion that downtown property lay in the hands of absentee owners devoted to indifference and neglect. We helped change this notion when our title search of the properties showed that downtown owners were mostly locals. Another big change occurred when Bill Cook let it be known that he intended to invest in the downtown because of its economic potential.

After the Graham Hotel project, CFC and other businesses undertook several important enterprises in close cooperation with the city. For example, during my administration the city built a parking garage at College and Fourth, south of the square. The garage served as an incentive for Cook's massive redevelopment of the square's south side: Fountain Square Mall, an interior mall with over a dozen buildings and a covered walkway to the garage. This and other downtown projects received additional incentives in the form of tax abatements and tax increment financing (TIF).

Not once did I doubt that we could revitalize the downtown. How could we fail? The square was so close to the university, only four blocks west of campus. At the center of the square stood a beautiful court house, vintage 1908—recently saved from the wrecking ball, restored with great care and skill, from its weathervane fish on the cupola right down to its basement. The neighborhoods surrounding the downtown were already a magnet for student residents. Most important, we had great popular support for a viable downtown. Once the movement started, its progress was steady.

Nevertheless, the struggle never ceased. The coming and going of new businesses would often raise doubts about the stability of the renewal equilibrium. But in the Fernandez administration, directly after mine, we began to see the results of the planning ordinance that allowed high density housing in the downtown. Student apartment buildings rose up on the skyline, together with upscale condominiums designed as non-student housing. The people had come, and business would serve them.

The Cook interests continued to invest heavily in the downtown, and played a key role in all major projects undertaken jointly. Foremost among those was the Showers Complex, which included the new City Hall. In the Showers project we worked again in a public-private partnership, this time with CFC and Indiana University.

Twice I was invited to take our plans for the Showers Complex to an architectural conference in Minneapolis. The Indiana Association of Cities and Towns had entered the plans of several Indiana cities in a competition among five midwestern states. We brought maps, photographs, and our Rails-to-Trails project. CSX Railroad had agreed that if it were to abandon the track that ran through the downtown, the city would have the first chance to buy the track. A competition winner was selected for each state, and our entry won for Indiana. The jury was most excited about the prospect of a Showers Complex, integrated and extended by means of a Rails-to-Trails project. The Showers Complex was completed as I finished my final term as mayor, and the B-Line Trail, an extension of our Rails-to-Trails project, was completed under the Fernandez and Kruzan administrations.

As noted above, our revitalization efforts did not go unrecognized. We won many awards, and hosted many visitors who wanted to learn how to revitalize their own communities. I was proud to carry our example to an international gathering, a Livable Cities conference in Charleston, South Carolina.

But what about the crowds in downtown Bloomington, as they shop at the Farmers' Market in the Showers parking lot on Saturday morning, or cruise music venues at the Lotus Music Festival, or wait before the Court House for the canopy of Christmas lights to come on? There could be no finer recognition of our efforts than the evident pleasure of residents and visitors as they enjoy and appreciate the vitality of downtown Bloomington.

NOTHING BY CHANCE

Poet Emily Dickinson's sister had a ready characterization of every inexplicable thing: It was "just a happen." None of this was just a happen. City employees knew a full court press when they saw one, and that was how they saw their drive to save the downtown.

No opportunity was overlooked. We helped to keep government offices downtown by putting our city police department into the Justice Building, a county facility. As we looked around for a new City Hall we kept at it until we found a downtown property ripe for redevelopment, the old Showers furniture factory. As the project was too much for the city to handle alone, we persevered until we found two capable partners, CFC and Indiana University.

Repeatedly we encouraged the county library to stay downtown. We encouraged both the Convention Center project and the Fountain Square project by helping to meet the need for parking. We changed zoning, setback and parking regulations to meet the needs of downtown merchants and residents.

The city gave an old city hall to the Bloomington Area Arts Council, conditional on a business plan and the wherewithal to manage the property. We renovated Third Street Park and provided a covered stage for performance arts in the downtown. On the square we pushed for facade improvements by paying for facade design, and providing small loans to execute the designs. We provided financial incentives: We made the downtown a Tax Increment Finance district, and offered tax abatements for downtown development.

City departments joined in. Public Works provided on-street trash cans, trash pickup, and traffic barriers for special events. Parks and Recreation helped with the commission's programming of downtown events. Redevelopment provided staff work, and other departments helped as needed.

No, it did not just happen. The results came from a long, deliberate team effort by countless city employees and business investors, all motivated by the vision of a vibrant downtown as a true source of pride, renown, and sound economic development.

Still, the struggle continues. The Monroe County Public Library, just two blocks east of the square, is a popular destination for all ages and a key part of the downtown nucleus. Yet, a few years after I left office library officials suggested that the downtown location be abandoned: The library was too small, they said, and a bigger one should be built in the suburbs, where cheap land would make it possible to accommodate more drive-in traffic, i.e., provide more space to park cars. At public hearings on the proposal, library officials were plainly surprised to find the public so thoroughly opposed to any move to the suburbs. We showed up, and we spoke our minds. The library expanded, but stayed where it was. A few years later, the public reacted similarly to a proposal to relocate the downtown post office. This time the protest failed, but it did manage to keep the new post office closer to the city center than it would have been. As I write, there is a movement afoot to move the hospital, now four blocks from the square, to wide open spaces several miles away. This proposal has also evoked a strong public protest.

This is what I meant when I wrote: "The great surge of downtown redevelopment began in the 1980s and continues to this day, but always in the face of opposing forces that would smash the vital nucleus of the city." These opposing forces will always be with us. Someone will always want to tear down or abandon the old court house, factory, library, post office, or hospital. Someone will always want to move something far from the center of town. Someone will always have some reason to do so. May our citizens always stand to defend the vital center of their city.

CHAPTER 13

Arts and Craft

Craft: *Skill in planning, making, or executing.*

THE JOHN WALDRON ARTS CENTER

In the early 1970s Rosemary Miller and a few of her artist friends began to dream aloud: How nice it would be to have a place of our own—nothing fancy, just a place to hang our art on the walls. Never one to start a project without some proper groundwork, Rosemary began to look around. She fastened her eye on the real estate market. She checked out every place that looked promising, on the market and off. She looked a long time, year after year, and along the way gathered more and more support for the object of her search: A home for Bloomington artists.

At last she came across the perfect location. There it was, on the southwest corner of Fourth and Walnut, right under her nose, right in the middle of town. The big limestone Beaux Arts building had started life in 1915 as City Hall. Fifty years later it became home to the Police Department, which stayed there until 1985, when the police moved into the new Justice Building. Even then the place was not quite vacant: At various times the city used parts of it as dormitory space for the fire station next door, as City Court, and as a repository of the City Clerk. The building was simply ideal. And on March 5, 1989, the city ended Rosemary Miller's long quest when we agreed to deed the property to the Bloomington Area Arts Council (BAAC), provided the council met several conditions.

One of those conditions was a great deal of money from the private sector—money needed for renovation, redesign, and operation. Her course now plotted, Rosemary went full ahead. Years later she told me: "People say they don't like to raise money, it's too hard to go out and ask. But it isn't hard. People really love to give money to save an old building." Translation: Rosemary, already a good beggar, became a world class one when it came to saving some worthy old building. "I went to Herman Wells. He didn't give me much, maybe $50. He never gave you much money, but he knew everybody. He gave me the name of a person nobody else knew, and said 'You should ask her. She will like this. And she has a lot of money.'" Her name was Cecile Waldron, wife of Charles, whose great-grandfather, John, had been a rainmaker in 19th-century Bloomington business. She did like Rosemary's proposal, just as Wells had said she would, and her donation of $375,000 was the boost that made the rest of the project possible. The conditions were duly met, and the property was deeded to BAAC on July 31, 1990.

The happy ending had my wholehearted blessing, but the project was actually a close run thing, and not the easy job it may have seemed to many. When Rosemary's proposal first came to my attention, the city administration was desperately short of space and needed all it could cobble together, including the space she wanted for the arts. One of the pieces fell into place when the City Court was folded into another judiciary unit and no longer needed a place in the old City Hall. More pieces fell into place when we built a new downtown fire station. That freed up both the fire station next to the old City Hall, and the station's old dormitory space. Additional donations from the private sector helped to provide the necessary financing, and volunteers pitched in with fund raising and the hauling/cleaning labor of site preparation. And, not the least of the pieces, we moved the city police to the Justice Building.

Rosemary's place for her and her friends to hang their art had grown much bigger than their initial dream. That modest place of their own came to include a third-floor performance space with over 100 seats. On the second floor one saw a grand hall, a gallery, a gift shop, a meeting room and offices. The first floor offered theater and gallery space, classrooms and dressing rooms. The old firehouse became home to Bloomington Community Radio (WFHB), the first community-owned radio in Indiana; it was funded separately from the Arts Center.

As the John Waldron Arts Center, it took its name from a once prominent citizen whose descendants had given the building new life. This institution has undergone some major changes since its dedication on October 4, 1992, including a transfer of financial and administrative responsibilities to IVY Tech Community College. But my mind's eye will always see it as Rosemary's baby.

THE MONROE COUNTY COURTHOUSE

One of Rosemary Miller's guiding principles for the good of the community is the unique value of historic preservation. Another is the indisputable role of the downtown as the vital center of city life. Others share these principles, but many do not. In the 1980s both principles were put to the test by a proposal to raze the county courthouse on the downtown square. To understand the passionate response to the proposal, it is helpful to know something about the history of Indiana courthouses, and the glory and decline of the one in Monroe County.

Glory Days

Our first courthouse was a two-room log cabin a little south of the present Courthouse Square. Our second, built in the period 1819-1826, was a two-story brick building with a tower. It occupied the present square, originally a cornfield, donated by David Rogers in 1818. Some authorities say its only surviving element is a moving part that now sits atop the courthouse dome, the weathervane fish familiar to all locals.

That fish story is probably not quite true. When the present dome was repaired in 2007, close inspection showed the fish to be a hollow welded structure, apparently brass, with black glass eyes and a dent in one side. Mounted and moving freely on suspiciously modern ball bearings, the fish was four and a half inches thick and eleven and a half inches tall—sixteen inches, counting the fins. Its length was five feet nine inches from nose to tail fin tip. The original fish was reportedly copper, gilded in 1884, and only three feet nine inches long. It seems that the original, which was blown down at least once, was probably replaced at least once by a bigger fish. To learn the quicksilver nature of historical "fact" one need only examine the "Courthouse Fish" folder in the Monroe County Library and its conflicting tales of fish provenance.

Our third courthouse was built of locally quarried limestone in 1906, 1907, 1908 or even 1910, depending on the source. According to journalists of the day, ground was broken on May 10, 1907, to the accompaniment of Masonic ceremony. Architect Marshall Mahurin would design the building, and the Henley Stone Co. would provide the best quality oolitic stone. The dome would be copper, with round vents incorporated in the design. The builders, Caldwell and Drake, of Columbus, Indiana, had the West Baden Hotel to their credit.

The new courthouse was dedicated on Saturday, July 4, 1908, and quite a day it was. A photograph shows gobs of horse-drawn vehicles clustered around the square. The celebratory crowd was inflated by a reunion of Spanish-American War veterans. Fine speeches were made, and a political celebrity was there: Congressman James E. Watson, a man so popular that he was obliged to eat three dinners that day laid on by three different organizations. There were fireworks, ice cream and a merry-go-round, but no drunken displays to spoil the celebration. A balloonist had waited patiently for the wind to calm down, and finally made his ascent at 6:30 p.m. It was another great day for Bloomington, what with its first sewer system and its first brick paving of city streets and sidewalks.

Of course someone had to pay the piper. Oscar H. Cravens listed those who would pay the most in the *Weekly Courier* issue of July 7, 1908. In summary, the cost of the new courthouse would be borne mainly by taxes on forty-three stone companies, five banks, and a group of ten "others" peppered with such familiar names as Showers, Gentry, Wicks, Buskirk, Waldron and Matthews.

The building itself was a thumping success. Numerous photos and descriptions reveal a handsome Beaux Arts design with Ionic and Egyptian columns, stained glass, and carved classical figures. A German artist, Gustav Brand, painted ten murals. He also provided a stained glass window, with American eagle, lighting the south stair landing.

In the final quarter of the nineteenth century—the state's great age of courthouse construction—Indiana architects strove to outdo one another. About two thirds of the ninety-two county courthouses went up in that period. Those buildings reflected a taste for the grand and the graceful that carried into the first third of the next century.[1] But as the twentieth century drew to a close many of the ninety-two became crowded, decayed or out of date. A few counties chose to tear them down and replace them with modern designs, but most chose to keep, restore, and adapt the old buildings. Now taken for granted, the proposal to restore our own great building in its period of decay was quite controversial at the time, and another close call for the city.

Decline and Dilemma

Reporter Carolyn Kramer told how the courthouse story had unfolded in Bloomington.[2] Her chronology began with a 1971 report of rainwater in the walls of Superior Court III. It was a story of peeled paint, cracked plaster, and plastic covers for the roof and dome. To County Commissioner Bill Hanna, no permanent repairs seemed possible.

In 1972 the County Commissioners proposed that the courthouse be torn down and replaced by a city-county building. As they had no funds, they took no action.

In 1977 the Commissioners petitioned for a bond to finance the necessary repairs, but the petition was defeated by a citizens' remonstrance petition. Commissioner Warren Henegar blamed the remonstrance on opposition from people in the downtown area. In 1978 a Monroe County grand jury found the courthouse in disrepair, its employees forced to work in cramped quarters. Commissioner John Irvine called the sixty years of neglect and deterioration a "crime."

Kramer's report continued. In 1980 the Commissioners replaced the roof for $150,000, but broken drainage pipes continued to leak water between the walls. They tried another bond drive that ended in defeat, this time ". . . at the hands of a new citizen's group," the "Save Our Taxes Committee." Also defeated was a plan to build an underground extension and make a public plaza of the ground level area.

The public gave voice in a barrage of letters to the *Herald-Telephone* (later the *Herald-Times*). On January 8, 1980, August W. Eberle called the courthouse in its present condition an architectural nightmare and a "hysterical" landmark. He went on to say we should tear it down and build a new one that would last at least two decades, or maybe we needed a building to house both county and city governments.

On January 12 another letter writer, Ivan Clark, mused about the commendable men who ordered the construction of the courthouse in 1906. However, the only part still enjoyed today was "A clock that strikes. Under a banner of reason let us now reduce that monument to a pile of rubble."

Maurice Endwright demurred in the January 13 *Ellettsville Journal*. He described the proposed renovation and expansion as a $7 million project. He referred to opponents who for fifteen years had repeatedly stifled all attempts to solve the problem, always in the name of some "better way." They had talked of building a new courthouse elsewhere, away from downtown, as other counties had done—but never with any savings achieved, as far as Mr. Endwright knew. They had talked of using the old one as a museum, or for restaurants or shops—things that had seldom become self-supporting. Towns that had made such changes typically ended up with deserted and dilapidated squares. In the interest of downtown preservation it would help to renovate other buildings besides the courthouse. The courthouse should be restored, and more space added, rented or leased. It should continue where it was as our seat of government.

Henry Ruh fired back at Mr. Eberle in the January 14 *Herald-Telephone*. He thought the courthouse was not as ugly as some persons seemed to think. Outdated, yes; it needed space and renovation that the planning committee could provide. Perhaps Mr. Eberle would prefer the "shoebox-on-end design" that any dunderhead (not meaning Mr. Eberle) with tee square and right triangle could provide, like those modern Chicago corncobs. And if it were that ugly, why would director Peter Yates put it in his movie, "Breaking Away"? Onions to Mr. Eberle.

On March 5 the Save Our Taxes Committee placed an ad in the *Herald-Telephone* urging the public to reject " . . . this costly courthouse project," whose total cost over 22 years, interest and all, could run to more than $13 million! The ad invited donations to the committee at 5522 West Popcorn Rd., Bloomington, Lester DeKoker, Chairman.

The letter writing discussion continued as Ruth C. Barnes weighed in on March 29. She praised the beauty of the dome's stained glass, its bronze, brass, wood and marble, its trees, shrubbery and statuary. She said that additional office space could be found around the square, perhaps in the restored hotel. And she noted the irreplaceable beauty of this central main attraction, the courthouse square.

On April 18 Virginia Parr praised the beauty of the courthouse trees and lawn, and scolded county officials for having proposed an underground addition that would have destroyed the trees and lawn. She identified herself as a member of the Save Our Taxes Committee.

An alternative solution had surfaced shortly before her letter. Mark Mandel, reporting for the *Indiana Daily Student* on April 16, noted that the County Council and Commissioners had agreed unanimously to seek appraisals of Graham Plaza, a stone's throw from the courthouse. The county might buy the building for $5.5 million to house county offices. The owner was CFC Inc., a subsidiary of Cook, Inc., of which Bill Cook was President. Mr. Cook had included a gift of $2 million for courthouse renovation in the proffered price of Graham Plaza. The county officials rejected as impractical Mr. DeKoker's alternative proposal to purchase the nearby J. C. Penney's building, partly because it promised no $2 million windfall. However, nothing came of all this promise. On May 18, 1980, the *Herald-Telephone* reported that the county had withdrawn its offer because the appraised value of Graham Plaza was too low to justify a $5.5 million bond purchase, the $2 million gift notwithstanding.

On March 5, 1981, readers of the *Indiana Daily Student* were treated to a description of working conditions in the Monroe

County Courthouse. Reporters Kevin Morgan and Janine Davis used stark terms: loud, crowded, unbearably warm in summer and winter alike. Workers had been forced to use the women's restroom for voter registration. Desks were shared. Cardboard boxes served as filing cabinets. A bump in a concrete floor steadily grew higher.

The year saw another bond drive. This one was supposed to raise $3 million for central heating and air conditioning, a new electrical system and window replacement. Commissioner Henegar thought it might succeed because the courthouse had been placed on the National Register of Historic Places. (Note: It had been there since 1976. The listing is an honor, but guarantees no protection.) However, he observed that county government was so structured as to lack power to effect change. "And that's the way the citizens want it."

But there was more to it than that. On May 20, 1981, *Herald-Telephone* reporter Kurt Van der Dussen described the fate of the $3 million bond issue. The issue had been pushed hard by an influential group, Bloomington Restorations Inc. (BRI). BRI led a two-month drive that gathered 3,457 signatures from county property holders on a petition to renovate the courthouse. Given such numbers, many were shocked when the County Council rejected the petition by a vote of 4-3. The majority thought the courthouse restoration was not sufficient; the real need was to deal not merely with one, but with two aging structures, the jail as well as the courthouse.

The Council rejection spared the Save Our Taxes Committee the trouble of a remonstrance against the bond issue, but BRI took umbrage. Its letter to the *Herald-Telephone*, dated July 16, apologized to all of its petition signers for its not having realized that an arbitrary Council decision could stymie community action. We would all see which was more durable: the courthouse, or the public careers of those who had voted against the proposal.

Pressure mounted in November, 1982. The state fire marshal ordered many expensive alterations to bring the courthouse into compliance with state standards and national codes. On the heels of the fire marshal a Monroe County grand jury found that the place should be vacated immediately as a fire and health hazard to courthouse employees.

Officials said they would have to wait for Odle-Burke Architects to work out the options and costs. According to the reporter, " . . . without saying it, (Commissioners President Charlotte) Zietlow, (and County Councilmen) Anderson and Wagner all seem leery of renovating the present courthouse." Zietlow noted that the replacement cost of heating, electrical and plumbing systems, and other needed alterations, would come to more than $2 million. "We don't have the money right now and I don't know where we'd get it. We could not do a bond issue strictly for this. It would be irresponsible." Anderson said, "The simplest and cheapest way is possibly to tear it down and build it right here." Wagner, mindful of the cost to the county's next generation, advocated the use of " . . . good, sound business judgment."[3]

In that same issue of the *Herald-Telephone*, citizen Paul Carmony disagreed in a letter to the editor. He thought it unbelievable that so many would advocate the razing of the courthouse. Expanding needs might be met by building an annex, as some counties had done. Just talk to the citizens of Anderson: They demolished their old building because they thought it intolerable, but found its replacement a troublesome eyesore that required huge sums just to keep it from falling down.[4]

Soon the officials would end over ten years of piecemeal planning, band-aids, and dither and echo his call. On November 14 *Herald-Telephone* reporter Dave Hancock announced the consensus of Monroe County officials on a comprehensive solution to their three salient problems: the courthouse, the jail, and insufficient space. They would restore the courthouse for office use. They would build a new facility for law enforcement offices, courts, and jail.

The Commissioners, council and members of the county holding corporation, meeting in executive session, mostly supported the plan. Zietlow indicated her support, but pointed out ". . . some disagreeable aspects." For example, the restoration would have to tear out part of the second and third floors to recreate the original rotunda from floor to dome, and would thereby reduce useable area. She added that each plan had its drawbacks, and urged prompt action.

Architects estimated the initial cost of the project at $13.7 million, of which Zietlow took $2 million as the cost of courthouse restoration. As the restoration would require a general obligation bond, it was vulnerable to the kind of remonstrance that had defeated previous proposals. Mary Baker, of the Save Our Taxes Committee, warned that the commissioners had ignored her group's alternative proposals. Zietlow soft-pedaled the additional cost to taxpayers.

However, by now it was plain that the issue had passed from purely local control. Mary Dieter, of the *Louisville Courier Journal*, had written about the jail a few days before, on November 10. She reported a suit against the county, filed by former inmates, about conditions at the jail. Grand jury recommendations might lack punch, but the adverse report from the state fire marshal commanded the full force of law.

The pot was stirred again when Bill Cook offered to renovate the courthouse for $2 million. For another $450,000 he would renovate the nearby Curry Building for county use. The *Herald-Telephone* related details on December 2. Cook said we had wasted twenty years on debate; it was time to act. His crews would strip out the inside, and replace cramped offices with fewer but larger spaces to be partitioned as needed. They would restore the original rotunda from first floor to dome, replace windows, insulate outer walls, install new plumbing, heating and electrical systems, build another stairway, replace the elevator and add another. Cook attorney Steve Ferguson suggested several ways to finance the project.

Resolution and Restoration

Early the following year, some of the pressure dissipated. On February 13, 1983, the *Herald-Telephone* disclosed that the state fire marshal's office would give the county until June 1 to bring the courthouse into compliance with state standards. Back in November the order had given the county thirty days.

Conflicting factions suddenly seemed more cooperative. On February 14 the paper reported that the commissioners had launched a public fund-raising campaign. Its purpose was to raise as much as $2.2 million to renovate the courthouse. Lester DeKoker, Chairman of the Save Our Taxes Committee, announced his support of the campaign. These contributions, deductible from federal income tax, would suppress property taxes. Commissioners President Zietlow praised DeKoker for having suggested the campaign.

By February 23 two hundred sixty-eight dollars had come in, including twenty-five dollars from former Mayor Frank McCloskey. The figure had climbed to three hundred five dollars by March 7, and five hundred twenty-six dollars and sixty cents by March 26. On April 5 the *Herald-Telephone* announced a "Save the Courthouse Rally" on the courthouse lawn. It would feature the Bloomington Community Band, speeches by Commissioners President Zietlow, Mayor Tomi Allison, County Council President Norm Anderson, and Save Our Taxes representative Lester DeKoker. Also on tap were hot dogs, soft drinks, ice cream, buggy rides, buttons, banners and T-shirts. On April 9 the paper printed a letter from Mr. DeKoker asking the public to contribute.

On May 23 reporter Van der Dussen declared the fund-raiser a "spirited success." At the auction Mayor Allison paid eighty-five dollars for a ride on the Oliver Winery hot air balloon. "My husband has always wanted to go up in that balloon; whether I go is another question." (Note: Both went up, and had a pleasant flight early one Sunday morning from Bloomington to Spencer.) At the dunk tank, *Herald-Telephone* columnist Greg Dawson fell in on four straight pitches. The pitcher was a female McDonald's employee with pinpoint control. She claimed revenge for Dawson's recent criticism of McDonald's failure to serve tomato slices with its hamburgers. A report the following day estimated that the effort had raised between $3,000 and $4,000 for the restoration fund.

The next day, June 24, 1983, the *Herald-Telephone* printed the restoration timetable. Work would begin in December and end in twelve to eighteen months. Architects Odle-Burke estimated the restoration cost at $1.8 million; moving, legal, and other costs would raise that total to about $2.5 million. The fund drive had reached $6,908.

Officials would soon begin a long, elaborate dance. Signatures on the pre-bond petitions were to be verified by June 27, legal notices posted in early July. The advertisement of the issue in late July would start a 30-day remonstrance period; the project would die if remonstrance signatures outnumbered restoration signatures. If the remonstrance failed, the county treasurer would meet with state officials to certify pre-bond petitions. Bids would be advertised in early September, the bonds printed in October. The bond sale would close in November, bids would be awarded, and the work begun soon after.

Officials would recede as builders surged in to tear out interior walls, add a stairway, and all the rest. Each floor would hold offices: Recorder, Assessor, Extension Agent, and Veterans' Affairs on the first floor; Auditor, Treasurer, County Attorney, and County Computer on the second; and Commissioners, Plan Commission, Surveyor, Engineer, and Highway Department on the third, which would also have a public meeting room to replace the Circuit Courtroom. County courts and related offices would move into the projected Justice Building, a block north at Seventh and College.

The new Justice Building would also house the new county jail, and new headquarters for county and city police. Why the city police? I had already offered to join with the county in the construction of a new city-county building as a way of meeting both our space needs. County officials had rejected my offer, but it remained important to affirm the city's financial and moral support. Accordingly, we agreed to put the city police into the Justice Building, and paid for the move with city bonding money. As a result, we had to delay for several years the building of the new city hall that we needed so desperately.

Advocates of restoration began to breathe easier. Still, there were warnings about the difference between a best laid plan and a done deal. On July 15 the *Herald-Telephone* ran an editorial that urged citizens to support the courthouse project, and not to support a remonstrance petition. On July 30 *Herald-Telephone* reporter Bill Reinhard noted that Lester DeKoker had petitioned the State Board of Tax Commissioners against the issuance of bonds to restore the courthouse. DeKoker explained that he supported the saving of the courthouse, but only on a cash basis. He did not say whether his Save Our Taxes Committee would mount a remonstrance campaign against the bonds.

The situation began to clear in October. The State Board of Tax Commissioners approved the sale of $2.5 million in bonds for the restoration project. The DeKoker group considered a suit against the state board on the grounds that the county had misrepresented the costs, but indicated that this would be its final opposition. There would be no remonstrance. On October 4 the *Herald-Telephone* reported that the state had rejected the

DeKoker petition. County Commissioners President Charlotte Zietlow and Mayor Tomi Allison reported progress on an agreement to set up a city-county police headquarters in the new Justice Building. Financial details remained to be negotiated.

The courthouse closed its doors on November 19, 1983. Bids were opened, relocations progressed, contracts were awarded and signed. On December 31 Van der Dussen reported on the auction of courthouse items, and noted graffiti and a poem scrawled on walls that would soon be razed. The poem:

> *Dirty walls*
> *Smoke-filled halls*
> *Stopped-up sinks*
> *Bathroom stinks*
> *Worn floors*
> *Battered doors*
> *Broken glass*
> *But lots of class*
> *County's soul*
> *Time's toll.*

Decades later Rosemary Miller, who had led BRI in its drive to restore the courthouse, offered some personal reminiscences. "The old courthouse on courthouse square was a mess, leaky and smelly. I began to hear that the authorities wanted to build a new courthouse way out on the edge of town. I didn't think that was such a good idea. I was talking to a professor friend of mine. He thought they should knock it down and build a parking lot in its place. I thought that was the worst idea I had ever heard. Knock down that beautiful old building? No way, not if I had anything to say about it. I started to talk to my friends, and found they felt the way I did: It's a wonderful building, the heart and soul of the city, and we have to fight to save and restore it. If the developers have their way, they will put every government building out on the edge of town with a parking lot in front. No way!"

She added that she had never bothered much with county officials. She would talk to them if she happened to see them, but she never depended on them. "Oh, they would agree with me and say yes, that's a good idea, but they never offered any real support. They didn't dare get out on the limb for anything that might cost money and annoy their tax averse public."

Rosemary Miller saw the courthouse restoration as a private initiative on behalf of the public, like the Waldron Arts Center. Without that push, neither might have happened.[5]

CHAPTER 14

Parks and Recreation

I came into office with some clear ideas about parks. My residence in California, Ann Arbor and Bloomington had taught me that parks programs could greatly affect the livability of any community. I thought of community as an inclusive entity that embraced every member of every neighborhood. From my experience on City Council I knew that our parks facilities had long been neglected for lack of money and lack of political will to raise taxes. But I also knew of a strong contingent of park supporters in both the community and the City Council. The need and the opportunity were crystal clear.

Where could we get the money for the necessary improvements? There were various possibilities. We could raise user fees. We could use park money more efficiently. We could raise taxes or float bonds for improvements. As the city was already administering the county parks programs, why not propose a county-wide parks district with taxing authority?

What did we have for assets? A major one was property owned by City Utilities. The city had acquired the land for Twin Lakes, Leonard Springs, Lake Griffy, and Lake Lemon over the years because of our continuing need for a supply of water. In addition, land might be given to the city by forward-looking real estate developers and industries, by railoads abandoning old tracks. There was also City Utilities' right-of-way land. Other major essentials were the knowledge, drive and creativity of city employees in Public Works, the Comptroller's office, and the Utilities and Parks departments. Our most important asset was citizen support. Many innovative programs came from suggestions from the public.

Some of the possibilities never panned out. Our proposal for a City/County Parks District failed partly because the county residents most in favor of parks programs were already being served by city parks. In addition, the state law that provided for a county-wide district aroused county opposition because the law specified a city majority among members of the joint park board. Expenditures on a new jail had already required a recent rise in county taxes. The result was a negative climate of opinion in both county government and citizenry against more taxes and a possible "take over" by the city. Big losers were county residents who happened to live in the city—the only taxpayers burdened with the administrative cost of two parks departments rather than one.

Environmental problems cropped up on land owned by City Utilities. Lake Lemon was threatened by eutrophication caused by pollution, but we lacked jurisdiction over some of the polluters because it was Monroe or Brown County that had jurisdiction over their lake-front property. Lake Griffy was threatened by development. Twin Lakes became a problem when the state ordered that the lake dam be breached for safety reasons.

Planning turned out to be the key. Frank Ragan, newly appointed head of our Parks Department, started with an inventory of park facility conditions. He followed up, in conjunction with the joint city-county parks board, by financing the design of a county-wide parks plan. The plan was designed in such a way that if a county-wide parks district did not materialize (as it did not), the plan could be separated into two workable parts, one for the city, one for the county. The city's part was a five-year plan to guide our park improvements in facilities and revenues.

Simultaneously, we included park needs as we updated the city's master plan.

The latter incorporated new plans for the Jackson Creek Watershed, the Southwest Quadrant, and neighborhood enhancement. They included future trails in old railroad tracks and Utilities rights-of-way. Park improvement was also involved in conservation plans for Lake Lemon, Lake Griffy and Cascades Park. Financial considerations were always there: planning to increase revenues; an open space acquisition fund; a cumulative capital fund; and a Park Foundation Fund to receive gifts of land and money. By 1995, the year I left office, we had an Urban Forest Plan to replace dead trees on city property.

The story of parks and recreation in the city of Bloomington is a very big one. I hope in these next pages to give due credit to the many players who enacted the story.

THE PARKS OF BLOOMINGTON

I learned something of the special meaning of Bloomington parks in 1965 when several citizens, led by Reverend Marvin Jones, organized the Community Development Conference (CDC) on the city's West Side. Our purpose was to encourage low-income people to become involved in politics so as to gain more control over their own lives.

Because our CDC members expressed a strong interest in affordable family entertainment, we sought to provide free entertainment in the Ninth Street Park. We recruited a superb volunteer force among Indiana University musicians. Other recruits formed a puppet theater that became the forerunner of Bloomington's famous Puck Players. Such programs drew big crowds to the Ninth Street Park. Their success led us to host a summer camp on I.U. property at Lake Lemon for our own children and children from the West Side's Crestmont area.

Years later, when I became a member of the City Council, I found three persons of influence who shared my notions about the function of community recreation. One was Edna Ballinger, a member of the city's Parks Board. Another was Pam Service, a member of City Council. Third was another member of City Council, Republican Lloyd Olcott, formerly on the Parks Board and always a staunch supporter of all things Park.

Our concept of parks programming went beyond sports. Parks are for everyone: singles, families, young, old, the rich and the poor. Parks should be places of relaxation and refreshment. All of us should benefit from both the natural beauty of our community, and such amenities as we ourselves provide. With its support of numerous festivals, the Parks Department made an extraordinary contribution, largely unrecognized, to the revitalization of our downtown.

Ours were strong voices for the inclusion of music, arts, theater, and nature study in parks programming. We thought that recreation was for the whole family, not just those who played sports. Pursuant to that concept, Parks initiated a Halloween event, Enchanted Forest, that proved immensely popular. We encouraged such programs as Music in the Parks. In 1988, after I became mayor, music professor Harvey Phillips, of Tuba Santas fame, persuaded me to have the city buy a mobile outdoor stage. Harvey pointed out that one of the reasons musicians needed such a stage was to protect their instruments from the weather. I was worried about the purchase price, $50,000, but the returns have far outweighed the cost. Harvey's stage has remained in constant use, much appreciated by musicians and their audiences.

Harvey's is just one brilliant example of citizen impact on the parks of Bloomington. During my days on the City Council two retirees, Tom and Polly Dixon, bore much responsibility for my success in starting our Clean Cities and Tree City programs. In turn, my experience with these programs led me to understand that if we were going to keep our treasured tree cover in town we would need a trained professional to take charge of city trees. As a result, I persuaded Mayor McCloskey to fund a city landscaper position. Lee Huss was hired to fill that slot. The city now plants over 200 trees per year, in recognition of which we receive our Tree City designation.

Some final examples that many may find surprising are the spectacular limestone benches in People's Park and Bryan Park. These came into being when citizen members of the City Arts Commission began to plan a limestone carving contest. As mayor I suggested that the carvings be park benches, and that the winning benches be put in the parks. My hope was for a periodical event, but the necessary organizational work proved to be too much for citizen volunteers to handle on a regular basis. Fortunately, the spirit of the event continues in the form of an Annual Limestone Symposium sponsored by the Bybee Stone Mill in Ellettsville.

NEW BROOMS

As a member of City Council I happened to make a disconcerting discovery as I reviewed the annual budget for our Parks Department. At least I thought it was disconcerting. What I found was that our then Parks Director had made it a practice to push the final month's expenses into next year's budget. This practice had obscured the fact that the Parks Department was chronically under-budgeted, and started each year in the hole. In plain fact, the parks budget had insufficient money to provide the programs the community wanted. Years of underfunding had driven our park facilities into a state of disrepair. That director retired, and Mayor Frank McCloskey hired Frank Ragan as the new Parks Director.

In the budget hearings of 1983, Ragan told City Council that necessary repairs to the Bryan Park pool would cost $200,000. Beyond that, he added, "There is so much that's needed to be done that this budget doesn't even touch."

Also in 1983 I was elected mayor by the Democratic precinct committeemen. That gave me less than one year in office to decide whether to treat park programming and its cost as campaign issues in the next mayoral election. To do what needed to be done, we would have to raise a lot more money—to go for the full amount of parks bonding allowed by the state. As the bond would be subject to remonstrance, it could become a political issue. We would have to collect enough signatures in favor of the bond to ward off a remonstrance that could kill the bond proposal.

As the reader knows, all politicians are leery of any tax increase. They are especially hesitant to let such an increase become a campaign issue. Still, we knew of exceptionally strong community support for parks. Accordingly, we decided to frame parks funding as the center piece of our campaign promises; we would take our citizens at their word and fund the parks system they said they wanted. And we were right. I won the election.

MONEY

It would take money to increase park programming, and good financial planning. The city employees who bore the burden of that planning were Public Works Director Pat Patterson (followed by Ted Rhinehart); Comptroller Betty Merriman (followed by Chuck Ruckman); Legal Counsel Harriet Lipkin (followed by Linda Runkle); Utilities Director Mike Phillips, and Parks Director Frank Ragan (followed by Norm Merrifield). They worked out the details, and we put the plan into effect.

State law permits a city to set aside money in a "cumulative capital fund." This is money that the city sets aside each year within a departmental budget, with the intention of financing some future project. In 1984 we began to assemble our financial plan by starting a cumulative capital fund for the parks. This enabled us to repair Bryan Park Pool right away, and add a water slide the following year. The water slide increased the pool's attendance, income and excitement. I got in on the excitement myself at a pool party for city employees. One slide ride was enough for me.

As explained above, our proposed City/County Parks District with its own taxing authority failed because of opposition on the part of county officials and citizens. In the end, county officials moved to set up their own parks department. Although the move severely strained their relations, city and county officials cooperated later on the development of the county's Karst Farm Park. And there was much the city could do on its own.

With the regular parks budget of 1984 we installed an elevator in the Older Americans Center, built a jogging trail at Winslow Sports Complex, and added one hundred parking spaces at Lake Griffy. We started the Bloomington Community Gardens program on Highland, another project inspired by citizen initiative. For years the city had bought seeds for Ms. Willie Streeter, who in turn gave them to people for their own gardens. Now the city would supply the land and plough it for the gardeners.

Except for the elevator installation, we did all of these projects with in-house labor, thanks to extraordinary cooperation among the Parks, Public Works, and Utilities departments. Each of these units had special skills, materials and equipment that, if used cooperatively, could and did stretch the money available for each unit's assigned job. I did my best to encourage an attitude of mutual trust by promising that the end result would be a fair division of opportunities among the different departments. Not without a certain amount of haggling, department heads always rose to the occasion, giving the city a highly unified, highly productive work force.

In the same year, 1984, we started the approval process for the County Option Income Tax, a tax that would help both our overall city budget and our parks program. With so much university property off the tax rolls, local government was habitually short of tax funds. Even our major industries were outside the city. A local option income tax would be a great help, but we would have to sell the idea, first to City Council, then the other taxing units in the county. City staff spent hour after hour in preparing the necessary background information. I spent hour after hour in presenting the information to the parties concerned, and much friendly persuasion. At last it came together in 1989, when all of the necessary units of government added their support to the County Option Income Tax.

Frank Ragan's analysis of park requirements had indicated the need for a bond issue to the tune of $3.8 million. The bond issue would include the cost of several crucial renovations. In need of attention were Frank Southern Center (including improvements to the lobby and the skating rink's pro shop); West Side Community Center, Ralph Mills and Bryan Park pools; Cascades Park (including lights for softball fields and a golf course club house); Third Street Park and Ninth Street Park. These renovations would also include an Arts and Crafts Center at Upper Cascades Park and expanded recreational programming for all ages. Tennis and other facilities would be upgraded including new playground equipment in every park and new softball fields. We would stabilize the shore line at Lake Lemon's Riddle Point. We would work with the county on a plan for soccer and football fields at Karst Farm Park. Incidentally, in their dogged pursuit of water, past city officials had seen our karst topography render several locations useless as sources for city water. However, we made these leaky reservoirs at Leonard Springs, Twin Lakes, Griffy Lake, Lake Lemon, and Wapahani into excellent sites for parks (and mountain biking, in the case of Wapahani). To execute these ambitious plans, we had to have public approval of a very big bond issue.

We went all out in our bond drive campaign. We enlisted everyone we could in City Hall and the community, and asked the support of the most active park users. We collected so many signatures in favor of the bond that it would have been very hard to top our numbers, and there was no remonstrance. It was a solid victory for the parks.

COST, REVENUE, AND SAVINGS

In 1987, when we set up our five-year master plan for the parks, we took care to include ways to increase revenues. For example, one of our studies had shown that the vast majority of Riddle Point users at Lake Lemon, a city facility, lived outside both the city and the county. We knew in addition that the user fees in place at Riddle Point had fallen far short of operating costs. Accordingly, we thought that the sensible way to increase revenues was to raise user fees. As a result of our fee increase, in one year revenues rose by $50,000, and wrought a significant reduction in Riddle Point's operating loss. A user fee increase had a similar effect following our improvements of Cascades Golf Course facilities.

It would be a grave mistake to imagine higher user fees as the cure for all revenue shortfalls. Three examples are the Mills Pool, the Westside Community Center (later named the Banneker Community Center) and the Frank Southern Center (later named the Frank Southern Ice Arena). In the first two examples typical users simply could not afford an effective rise in user fees. However, I thought the facilities so essential to the community that I weighed in heavily to keep them open and operational. Frank Southern Center, whose users were relatively few but passionate, had several strikes against it: a short operating season, high cost per user, and outmoded ice-making equipment in need of expensive repair. The situation was sufficiently complicated that we appointed a study committee to make recommendations, and eventually devised a plan that kept the facility open.

At the same time that we were doing our best to analyze costs and raise revenues, we were also doing our best to cut costs. The computer revolution, then in its early days, turned out to be a major cost saver. The centerpiece was our initiation of computerized registration for parks programs. When we saw how much staff time this could save, we gave Parks a high priority for access to computer technology and training in its use.

ENVIRONMENT

Have you ever tried to mow a lake? The story begins with two big headaches called Lake Lemon and Lake Griffy.

Bill Jones, a professor in the I.U. School of Public and Environmental Affairs, identified major pollution threats to both of these lakes, former water supplies for the city. We were determined to recover these assets as a valuable part of our commons, even though they had failed as city water supplies. It was Bill Jones who furnished the basic scientific research we needed to understand the threats and how to meet them effectively. His scientific study of both lakes provided the basis for the city's solution to the problem. We would create Griffy Nature Preserve and the Lake Lemon Conservancy District, comprehensive measures that could save both bodies of water. The job entailed a great deal of work on the part of the Legal, Planning, Utilities, Comptroller, and Parks departments.

Lemon presented the more difficult problem. For one thing, it spanned two counties. For another, most of its shoreline was private property whose owners held conflicting views. We had to devise some sort of governance to assess property owners for the upkeep of the lake. The upkeep itself was no small challenge. Pollution and the consequent eutrophication had encouraged a vigorous growth of weeds that had to be mowed with regularity: There would be no boating without mowing.

When the lake ceased to be even a backup water supply, the property owners' interest in the lake grew still bigger than the city's, and we grew still more determined to find a workable assessment mechanism. Voluntary payment for upkeep was not working. We could not enforce compliance on residents of Brown County. The answer was a comprehensive conservancy district, but the property owners had to vote it in—as they finally did, in 1995. This effort represented much devoted work from both our Legal Department, and our Utilities Department led by Mike Phillips.

To have a true notion of the kind and amount of work involved, the reader should understand how one creates a conservancy district in Indiana. State law says that landowners can organize a special taxing district to solve problems related to water management. To establish a district, one must circulate a petition in the area to be included, and file it in the Circuit Court of the county having the most land in the district. The petition must have the approval of at least 30% of 1000 freeholders, or 15% of 1001 to 5,000 freeholders, and so forth. Once approved or disapproved by the state's Natural Resources Commission, the conservancy petition goes back to the Circuit Court for a hearing on the establishment of the district. If the court does establish the district, the County Commissioners appoint the first Board of Directors, after which the district freeholders elect the Board at an annual meeting. The Board obtains an engineering report that sets out the general purposes for which the district was formed. The report is to include a physical description of the district, maps, drawings, preliminary estimates of the cost of improvements, and copies of agreements about financing, construction, operation, and maintenance. But before the Board can set the work going, the plan must be approved by the Natural Resources Commission and the Circuit Court. The Conservancy District is a taxing district. It can pay for its improvements by receipt of gifts, government funds, sale of services arising from the district, assessments collected from land that receives exceptional benefits from the operation of the district, or assessments for maintenance and operation.

Griffy was simpler, but problematical enough. It occupied Utilities property that often silted up. Housing encroached on the delicate ecology, with several rare species of plants, that surrounded the lake. We needed a long-range, development-proof solution that would still permit hiking and row boating. Utilities, Parks, and Planning departments worked it out together. We made the area more accessible to the handicapped, and in 1991 secured its lasting protection as a nature preserve. A nature preserve is simpler than a conservancy district. Indiana's nature preserve system dates from 1967, when the state acted to provide permanent protection for important natural areas, living museums that contain a record of our natural and historical heritage. Such an area becomes a preserve with the agreement of the land owner, the Department of Natural Resources, and the Natural Resources Commission. Once dedicated, it is protected in perpetuity from development that would harm its natural character.

When the state told us that we had to breach the Twin Lakes dam to rid the houses downstream of the dangerous threat of a dam break, a Parks employee suggested that the drained lake might have the makings of a softball park. The utilities-owned land was in a flood plain, not suitable for housing. However, it turned out to be perfectly suitable as a site for four lighted softball fields. As such, Twin Lakes Sports Park has drawn both many tournament teams from far and wide, and countless local players. The suggestion originated with Mick Renneisen, our Sports Division Director, who later became a distinguished long-time Director of the Bloomington Parks and Recreation Department.

OF PARKS AND PLANS

A good way to expand a park system is to incorporate the system in the city's Master Plan. In Bloomington, the incorporation of parks in our planning encouraged the acquisition and gifts of land for future parks and trails. We tried to make it easy and advantageous for property holders to give us land for parks development, and we liked the results.

Our planning for the Jackson Creek Watershed alone resulted in two parks and a trail. Later administrations developed Sherwood Oaks II, Olcott Park, and Jackson Creek Trail. In the Southwest Quadrant of land outside the city, Thomson Community Park and Clear Creek Trail came out of our planning.

On a quite different scale, Neighborhood Enhancement Plans enabled us to develop neighborhood "pocket" parks from small land parcels received as gifts. These included Parkwood East and Latimer Woods.

How did we pay for all of this? First off, we took advantage of regular infrastructure planning to help provide the roads and utilities needed to service parks. We used cumulative capital funds and the city's Open Space Acquisition Fund. And we had our Parks Foundation Fund, which provided a tax-friendly mechanism by which we could accept gifts of land and monies for parks.

No account of Bloomington parks would be complete without special mention of City Councilman Lloyd Olcott as the prime mover behind our first Rails-to-Trails. Lloyd worked incessantly with the Parks Department and the owners of the railroad spur. The product was so popular that in planning the new City Hall we incorporated the CSX rail that connected Country Club Road to Ninth Street Park (renamed Ernie Butler Park in 2003). Because CSX was still using the property, our legal department worked hard, for more than a year, for the first right of refusal when and if CSX decided to sell. The city secured this right as my time as mayor came to an end. It fell to two subsequent administrations to purchase and develop the B-Line Trail.

It was Mike Phillips, Director of City Utilities, whose foresight gave us our Clear Creek Trail. He suggested that as long as Utilities had to get right of way for a new utilities line, we should also negotiate permission to build a trail on the right of way that could connect with Rails-to-Trails. Accordingly, he sought grants to initiate a process that finally came to completion in the next administration. And the trail became our 2.4-mile Clear Creek Trail.

Planning paid off in a big way with the gift by Thomson, Inc., of forty-eight acres in an area that had no infrastructure. Thanks to the cooperation of City Utilities, Public Works, Planning, Redevelopment, and Parks we were able to provide a new park, affordable housing, and infrastructure improvements that encouraged development in an underdeveloped area next to the city.

As I look back on our development of parks and recreation, I recall over and over how much less we would have done but for the forward thinking of our department heads, their spirit of generous cooperation, and the help of community members. I think of the new parks and programs that came into being because community groups sought them. I think of the I.U. fraternity, Pi Kappa Phi, that co-sponsored the Winslow Woods playground for the handicapped. Kid City and Tots' Town, programs that grew from the needs of working parents and their children. Senior citizens who used so well the tiny amount of funding I provided to encourage Golden Age Radio. Special Olympics, Maplefoot Skate Board Park, the Teen Council's help with our programming for teenagers.

I know what parks have meant to the citizens of Bloomington, Indiana.

CHAPTER 15

Social Needs

AFFORDABLE HOUSING

Affordable housing and the plight of the homeless, prominent issues in my administration, seem never to go away. I remember an urgent phone conversation in my car on the road home from a meeting in Greencastle. Our corporation attorney thought I should know about a tent city that might soon be pitched in the park near City Hall. What should we do about it? The year was 1995. The same issue inspired a similar incident in a Bloomington winter fifteen years later.

In my administration we had used federal money to rehabilitate older houses for income-eligible families. That program had helped stabilize the town's supply of affordable housing, but we needed and wanted more.

In 1992 September had special significance for me as a month of tangible progress on the problem. Under the leadership of Redevelopment Director Chris Spiek we had worked out a plan to establish a Community Land Trust that would own a 29-lot subdivision, and sell the homes on the lots to income-eligible residents. Each resident would own a 99-year lease. An owner who chose to sell the property could pocket any equity, plus a small amount of appreciated value. However, under the terms of a deed restriction, the buyer must also be income-eligible. How did we pull this off?

Research had taught me the three elements in the cost of financing housing: the costs of land, money, and building. We decided to negotiate the lowest price for money and building materials, but pay the going rate for labor. A great surprise was how much we could reduce the total price by separating the cost of the house from the cost of the land on which the house stood. We found that if the buyer would own the house, but only lease the land, we could greatly reduce the price of our houses.

Lady Luck helped, with a big windfall of federal money that came to us in a most roundabout way. Indiana had been receiving Community Development Block Grant money, "pass through" federal funds intended for the benefit of low-income citizens. The feds objected when they discovered that the state had been parking these funds in the bank for six months so as to draw interest to state coffers. When a court ruled against that practice, as part of the settlement our city received $500,000. We decided to use it for affordable housing.

Another part of the story was infrastructure. It so happened that Thomson/RCA had given us land for a park, with the city to provide in return an access road, water, and sewer services. As we had already prepared the infrastructure for the park, we saw the ideal chance to acquire some adjacent land, suitable for housing, that could share that infrastructure.

Another key element was the cost of supplemental money. Through the hard work of banker Jerry Hays at Workingmen's Federal Savings and Loan we were able to supplement our funds, as necessary, at the lowest interest rate any human could find.

As a result of all this, we brought those houses in at the lowest market price.

Spiek wanted to have the homes ready for occupancy soon, the following spring or summer. Accordingly, his redevelopment department asked the plan commission to waive its normal second hearing. City planning went along, and recommended that the commission approve both final plan and waiver.[1]

When the houses came onto the market, they sold without delay for $55,000 to $85,000 each. Soon we acquired another small parcel next to the original land, and added another half-dozen houses. This project exemplified our standing policy, under which the city would create programs, but spin them off to other agencies for continued direction and management—in this case, to Housing Solutions, Inc.

I hoped that this novel example of affordable housing would stand as a model for further development. It did not. The original model fell prey to financial mismanagement. When Housing Solutions, Inc. went under, the land was sold to the home owners, the deed restrictions were lifted, and new mortgages were negotiated with private banks. The Housing Trust Fund still exists under the auspices of city government, but its potential lies dormant. To my regret, the tent cities erected in several subsequent winters have shown that much more work on affordable housing remains to be done.

HUMAN RESOURCES

County government has the taxing authority necessary to meet some of the social needs of its citizens. City government does not, but money isn't everything. Having worked with volunteers all my political life, I knew that much could be done with relatively little money, given the proper direction. I was fortunate to find in Sue Wheeler the perfect Director of Human Resources. In 1984, with a city budget of $132,000, she contrived to bring in $689,000 worth of grants to serve social needs of Bloomingtonians. Later, in 1991, she showed what she had learned. With a city budget of $200,000, she brought in $3 million.

To discover the city's social needs, we conducted assessment research and found that the top four needs were food, quality day care, housing, and medical care. Our method was to provide start-up help to appropriate service organizations, then spin the programs off. We did not want the city to administer programs; we wanted the city to be free to provide start-up help to other new programs. For example, we provided technical assistance to community grant writing, record keeping, and program organization and management. By means of the Volunteer Action Network, we provided information and referrals.

In addition, we worked with existing agencies. When the Mental Health Center wanted to build Hoosier House we helped with grant writing, as we did when Amethyst wanted a house, and when the Community Action Program (CAP) wanted to fund a new building. We worked with Public Health Nursing on the expansion of its clinic program, with Middle Way House on its Rape Crisis Center, and with Hoosier Hills Food Bank and Bloomington Dental Clinic.

Sue Wheeler played a major role in the creation of our Community Foundation. A city councilman, Jack Hopkins, had done a great deal to increase the city's contribution to not-for-profits, but we knew we needed more of their kind. It was Sue Wheeler's task to get the Community Foundation going, and she succeeded brilliantly.

The city started many new programs: Helene's House (homeless housing); Self Sufficiency (agencies working together to help welfare recipients become self supporting); Day Care Resources (for parents with young children); Cares (action for teens); and Emergency Shelter Grants. The city administered the Senior Citizens Nutrition Project, the Senior Citizens Drug Prescription Project, and the Child Care Food Program.

When the director of another county's Workforce Development Program got into trouble, Sue earned an above-and-beyond medal for stepping up to run the program for a short time. She served on a great many boards that dealt with a great many needs, ranging from education to corrections.

My personal interest in social needs led me to serve on boards concerned with self sufficiency and adult education. I thought we should pay more attention to the education of high school dropouts, that we should help people help themselves to rise out of poverty.

Sue Wheeler and her staff accomplished great things, but when I left office she lost her job to a friend of my successor. Something similar happened to Chris Spiek, my Redevelopment Director. Such bittersweet stories are a political commonplace, but I have never learned to take them with the calm expected of a seasoned professional.

CHAPTER 16

The Showers Project

When I took office City Hall overflowed with city personnel, but our space needs would have to take a back seat to more pressing ones. During my first campaign we kept an ear to the ground for what the public wanted us to accomplish, and soon after the election I gathered my department heads to hear their priorities. First in line was major road projects, followed by restoration of city parks, more fire stations, and better sewage infrastructure and equipment. We definitely needed a bigger City Hall, but other projects would have to come first. As its time approached, we began to see what the City Hall project would not be.

For several reasons we could not simply expand the present building. To enlarge the building's footprint would cut the space for parking, already scant, even further. It would cut into the small park south of City Hall—contrary to both our own policy, and a restrictive covenant against any encroachment on the park.

Also taboo was the thought of building upward. Vertical growth would add no parking space, and we soon found that the structure could not bear another story anyhow. To grow taller we would have to raze the place and start again from the ground up—not to mention the trouble and cost of temporary quarters while the brand new structure went up. We knew too that our Third Street City Hall would be a good place for the Police Department, itself in need of new quarters. The Third Street building, originally meant for the Police Department, had been appropriated by McCloskey's predecessor, Mayor Hooker, and declared City Hall. The police would be glad to reclaim it. All in all, it would be better to leave that place intact, and relocate.

To gather community advice and support, we formed a committee of citizens to tour City Hall and see working conditions for themselves. They were members of neighborhood associations, businessmen, Chamber of Commerce representatives, university officials and providers of social services. Many were astonished at what they found. We were using closets as offices. We had already been forced to move Parks and Recreation from City Hall to another building, and soon we might have to move other departments as well. The response was practically unanimous. We most certainly needed a new, bigger City Hall. And it had to stay downtown, given our revitalization policy.

If we needed a new City Hall, and it had to be downtown, where could it go? The ultimate answer came from an informal breakfast group that included Chuck Ruckman, City Comptroller; Bud Faris, owner of a downtown grocery store; and Bill Morrow, a downtown realtor. One day Chuck came into my office with his breakfast group's proposal. What about the old Showers furniture factory? It was in the right place, a few blocks northwest of the square. It was probably available, as Indiana University, its present owner, used it only for storage. It was certainly big enough. But its very size would be problematical, far too big for a City Hall. However, it might be just right for a three-way condominium shared by the city, the university and a private corporation, Cook Enterprises. It would still take a great deal of doing, but from that time on we had a practical working concept that eventually gave us both the restoration of an iconic Bloomington landmark, and a new architectural gem with nationwide acclaim.

HISTORY OF THE SHOWERS COMPANY

In 1856 a yellow fever epidemic prompted Charles Showers and his family to move north from Shreveport, Louisiana. Bloomington was not their intended destination; they settled there by various accidents of health and transportation, not design. In partnership with James Hendrix, Charles Showers made good money from the manufacture of coffins during the Civil War, after which the partners resumed the manufacture of wooden bedsteads and dressers. In 1867 Showers' two eldest sons, James and William, bought his interest in the firm and were soon joined by their younger brother, Charles. The next year James and William founded the enterprise that became the Showers Furniture Company of Bloomington, Indiana. They produced mainly beds, and three-piece bedroom suites equipped with plate glass mirrors made by the Nurre Company, which Showers eventually absorbed.

Over the next few years the company grew sporadically, waxing and waning with the general economy. Around 1880 it employed one hundred ten workers and produced about 1,350 bedsteads per week. Fire destroyed the factory in 1884, but before the year was out a new plant had arisen in the place that became its permanent home on Morton Street.

As a measure of the company's importance to the town, the city council provided half of the money for the construction of the new building. The reopening was a gala event, with handbills, speeches, music, and a flag-raising. The new plant had three separate buildings, spaced a hundred feet apart as a hedge against fire damage. In 1893 the company added space by connecting the three. In 1910 it was Bloomington's biggest employer; business boomed, thanks partly to the company's introduction of laminated veneer, a lightweight material much preferred to the old heavy solid-oak style.

In response to demand, the company built a new plant around the old even as the old one continued its production. Designed by Chicago architect C. H. Ballew, the new brick building had a saw tooth roof, hard maple floors and an extremely strong deck made of diagonal tongue-and-groove planking. It covered seven acres, and came to be known as Plant Number One. Soon about sixty percent of the nation's furniture production would come from Showers.

Plant Number Two went up in 1912, when the employees numbered about five hundred; a third building arose in 1915, by which time the number of employees had climbed to a thousand. By 1919 the company had introduced a popular line of kitchen cabinets and built Plant Number Four about sixteen blocks away, on a site later occupied by the RCA plant. A robust market inspired the construction of another plant in Burlington, Iowa, in 1920, and the acquisition of a chair factory in Bloomfield, Indiana, in 1924. The first item of furniture in a Sears catalog appeared in 1920; it was a suite from the Showers Furniture Company of Bloomington, Indiana.

The company was seen as a valuable community asset. It employed women liberally and paid good wages. It was one of the first companies to hire blacks early in the twentieth century. In its heyday it was perhaps the largest furniture maker in the world, with an entire floor of Chicago's enormous Merchandise Mart. At its peak in 1929 the payroll reached $1,571,000, with sales over ten million dollars. The company had a welfare department that ran the incentive-holiday programs; these programs gave workers time off for meeting specific production objectives, distributed Christmas gifts to employees, and organized entertainment—plays, dances, and concerts. It paid workmen's compensation, health and death benefits, and ran a company store where employees could buy food and dry goods at a discount. It sponsored a Boy Scout troop, gun clubs, basketball and baseball teams, a band and an orchestra, and provided an auditorium.

During the flush times the company enjoyed good labor-management relations. Union organizers had little success at

Showers. Bad economic times brought worse relations and a better climate for organized labor, but even then relations remained relatively placid.

The Depression of the 1930s brought hard times to Showers. It faced competition from southern manufacturers, who benefited from lower wage rates and cheaper access to furniture wood. It competed for labor with the local RCA plant, which offered higher wages, better benefits, and better working conditions.

The company struggled through the 1930s and got a brief lift from wartime commerce, but never really recovered. In the early 1950s, when Showers still had about five hundred workers, it was sold to Storkline, a Chicago manufacturer of children's furniture. In 1959 Indiana University acquired the building and used it as a storage facility.

Given the role it had played for nearly a century as one of Bloomington's biggest and best employers, a world industrial power, its history entwined with generations of Bloomingtonians, it is easy to understand the depth of affection so many of them felt toward Showers and its building. The company had been good to the town, to them, to their friends and relatives. It had left many fond memories. What a shame it would be to see the Showers building razed or neglected.[1]

PULLING IT TOGETHER

Long before Chuck Ruckman and his breakfast group, many designs on the future of Plant Number One had come and gone. During my first administration we asked a St. Louis architectural firm to come up with a design for five downtown revitalization projects. One of the five involved the conversion of the Showers building into a big indoor mall/hotel complex. The architectural sketches made the project seem attractive and plausible, but we soon learned our city was too small to support such a big development. In connection with one such proposal I toured the building with a group that wandered among great heaps of university stores that ranged from residence hall furniture to theatrical props. We tried to ignore unmistakable evidence that someone had taken a lot of trouble to arrange a number of dummies in suggestive poses and juxtapositions.

We knew about Showers. We appreciated its practical potential, and its emotional appeal. But our interest in the building remained dormant until Chuck Ruckman and his group saw its possibilities for the City Hall project.

As early as 1989 the university had explored Showers' potential as a research park. In July of that year I.U. Vice President John Hackett spoke to a reporter about starting work on a research park complex at Showers. Mike Davis, my Deputy Mayor, noted Hackett's remark as a plus for downtown revitalization, and so did I. We talked of moving City Hall to 7th and Morton, a place near Showers, but not of Showers itself as a site for City Hall. What we had in mind were the old creamery building of Johnson Dairy Products, and the Regester Center Parking Garage at 7th and College.[2] A few weeks later Hackett repeated the university's plan for Showers as a modern research park, but made no reference to any other possible players in the Showers renovation.[3]

By January 1990 two possible sites for City Hall had popped up in public discussion, the creamery and the parking garage.[4] City Council was divided between the two, as were others in the community. I had been publicly criticized by an outspoken member of my own party for keeping my own preference to myself in deference to the City Council. In fact I had already expressed a preference for the parking garage site because it was prominent, and near downtown.[5, 6] Unfortunately, that property was too small. To have enough parking and office space we would have to raze the existing structure and build higher than we could afford.

City Council moved toward a choice between the parking garage and the creamery. But before it could vote, I approached Indiana University with a proposal to lease space at Showers.[7]

Bob Barker, Showers Project Coordinator, recalled a 1990 conversation with Steve Ferguson, president of CFC real estate development. Ferguson said that CFC might like to buy one-third of the research park. The city had already said it might want part of the space in the research park for the new City Hall. In the summer of that year the I.U. Board of Trustees agreed to have Showers appraised and sold for development as a combined City Hall, research park and commercial space.[8] According to Barker, "What really put wheels on the project, though, was the fact that Tomi Allison came to me and said, 'Bob, what would you think if the city were to buy one-third of Showers?'"

In April 1990 City Council voted to create a holding company to help finance the building of a new City Hall and a downtown fire station. It would issue bonds to pay for design and construction. It would lease the buildings to the city, which would buy them back with money derived from the County Option Income Tax.[9]

Early 1990 saw much opposition to the City Hall project, but the controversy faded. By year's end the plan for a new City Hall in the old Showers building had widespread business and editorial support.[10, 11]

From that time on the development of the project resembled a complex mating ritual among the three key players. Linda Runkle, Corporate Counsel, handled all of the city's legal details. There was a seemingly endless series of meetings, buffered by Barker through a maze of turning points. A key moment came in the winter of 1991, when the City Council voted money to lease part of Showers for the development of a new City Hall.[12]

Big things happened in the next three years. By May 1992 the I.U. Board of Trustees had given Bloomington Advancement Corporation (BAC) an option to purchase Showers on the understanding that BAC would develop and renovate the property, lease about one-third back to I.U., and sell another third to the city and another as office space. (BAC was a not-for-profit group to promote economic development, responsible for the development of the Showers project.)[13] The same year a committee chose an architect. The committee had representatives from City Council, the Board of Public Works, Bloomington Municipal Facilities Corporation, and my office. The winning firm, chosen among several bidders, was Odle, McGuire and Shook of Bloomington.[14] The general contractor, also chosen among several bidders, was E.A. Wilhelm, of Indianapolis.

In the fall of 1993 City Council voted to issue a $9 million bond to finance the Showers purchase and renovation, whereupon I stood and applauded.[15] The next big news came a few weeks later, when I.U. sold the Showers building to BAC for $2.5 million. The city was to buy 66,000 square feet for use as City Hall, CFC about 65,000 to lease as office space. I.U. would lease 70,000 square feet for sublet as a research park.[16]

The Indiana Association of Cities and Towns chose Bloomington as an example. We would take our Showers Project to a charette in Minneapolis, with topographical maps, photos, and everything we knew about buildings in the Showers neighborhood. At the meeting a group of architects, engineers, landscape architects and city planners brainstormed suggestions for the development of the area. Later we returned for a similar treatment of our plans for the urban trail on the old CSX railroad tracks.

The ritual continued for two more years, a year longer than many experts had expected. Indiana University did not sign its lease until May, 1994. In the critical later stages it was Corporate Counsel Linda Runkle who ramrodded the city's part of the project. By then another major player was the chief architect, Christine Matheu, of Odle, McGuire and Shook. According to a newspaper report, I had said "When the construction actually starts, there will be such a shout of 'Hooray!' that it will be heard throughout the city."[17] In the same article, Christine Matheu's

Official opening of new City Hall November 3, 1995 (Murphy, Brand, Allison, Olcott)
(uncredited photo).

enthusiasm for the project leaped off the page. "Showers is a spectacular resource. The sheer amount of open space that it offers cannot be found anywhere else in Bloomington. . . .The lighting it offers is absolutely glorious." Inside the city's part of the building the City Council Chambers would rise to a second tier with a public balcony section that could seat 200. In addition to all of the city offices, and a big foyer with exposed timber beams and skylights, there would be six conference rooms and eight bathrooms. The complex would become a hub for the city, with a south plaza for outdoor markets and festivals. But before that could happen a mind-boggling number of details had to be settled. For example, one summer evening a number of us met in a Showers parking lot to compare alternative lighting fixtures. We fended off the phototropic bugs, peered upward and tried to decide which shape would go best with the building's night lines, color and texture.

In November 1995 the principals staged a gala opening reminiscent of the one in 1884, complete with 500 invited guests. They heard a steam whistle, much like the old factory whistle, blown to begin and end the festivities. There were speeches by BAC President Lloyd Olcott, Showers family descendant Robert Dillon, me, CFC officials Steve Ferguson and Jim Murphy, and I.U. President Myles Brand.[18] When it was done the *Architectural Record* sent a photography crew, and featured the building in a laudatory spread in its issue of February 1996.[19]

THE RESPONSE

The public loved it from the start. First-time visitors liked the ample parking right in front of City Hall. They liked the beauty of the landscaping and the brick entryway, the helpful receptionist in the foyer, and the color-coded doors that distinguished the departments and made it easy to find the one you wanted.[20]

A lot of careful planning had gone into the building. The architect based her interior design on interviews with workers in every department. She used this information to tailor each department's space to its particular needs. Our experience with the

Chancellor Wells and Mayor Allison in the new City Hall (undated, uncredited photo).

Congressman and former Mayor Frank McCloskey at the podium, Mayor Allison and James Allison. Dedication of new City Hall, November, 1995 (undated, uncredited photo).

old city hall, sadly lacking in windows, had left us especially attentive to lighting, and grateful for the natural light potential of the Showers building.

From the building's north side the site slopes nearly a full story to the southeast, stepping down in a series of terraces. The terrace "benches" were my idea. To encourage the public to gather there, we bordered each terrace with concrete strips that could function as seating. My inspiration for this intimacy between the public and their City Hall was our attractive Courthouse surround.

In addition, we saw that the brick steps leading up to the front entrance could be used for seating in the front plaza. Directly south of the steps we put a spacious parking lot where the Farmers' Market now takes place every Saturday from spring through fall. My hope was to provide temporary shelters for the market that could easily be taken down and re-erected, for interim use of the parking lot as seating for a big outdoor stage. However, the next administration chose to install a permanent shelter instead. The shelter is beautiful, but not readily adaptable to other uses.

In June, 1996—several months after the opening—a twelve-foot fountain was installed on the grassy plot in front. It was a vase-like structure, Indiana limestone, patterned after an ancient cistern. Its creator was a sculptor from Dallas named Brad Goldberg.[21] It was financed at a cost of about $200,000 by a plan co-sponsored by City Council members Pat Cole and Pam Service, whereby one percent of the cost of any new city building would be set aside to pay for artistic furnishings. Donations included forty-five tons of stone from Elliot Stone Co. and money from the Indiana Arts Commission, Bloomington Community Foundation, and PSI Energy.

Cole, herself an artist, guided the selection of the final design. Water spills gently over the lip of the cistern. It falls into a circular pool at the base, flows down a grassy slope through a serpentine trough and ends in a spiral coil.

The fountain sparked a controversy familiar to most advocates of public art. First came the criticism of any public outlay on any such useless frivolity as a fountain. Other critics, not necessarily opposed to public art, ridiculed the piece as inferior to certain fountains on the I.U. campus—all more expensive, all privately financed.

As the furor faded, the ultimate verdict appeared in a photograph taken at the fountain's dedication in July, 1996. The fountain is in the background among a crowd of spectators seated on folding chairs. From the base of the fountain a serpentine trough runs downhill to the foreground, where a five-year-old girl named Madeline Baumgartner faces the camera. Dressed for a summer dip, Madeline stands poised on one edge of the trough like a tightrope walker, arms stretched out and a smile on her face. According to the reporter, the water began to flow when the dedication ceremony concluded, whereupon the kids jumped in and had a good splash.[22]

Madeline Baumgartner, Showers fountain dedication, July 1996 (Snodgress, H-T).

CHAPTER 17

Planning and Zoning

My interest in local politics came from my concern about livability. We had bought our house in Elm Heights as much for the neighborhood as the house; its sidewalks encouraged walking. We could walk to the nearby campus for work or university culture, the children could walk to school or Bryan Park, we could walk to town or the county library. It was an old, established neighborhood with an attractive variety of ages, occupations, houses, flora, and fauna. All of these things made daily life more pleasant.

But all of these things needed protection. We soon found such neighborhoods imperiled by developers. University growth had brought many changes, some welcome, some not. As restrictions fell away, more students became free to live off campus, to bring their cars to the university. Developers saw a market for student housing in single family homes. In the 1970s a Democratic city council obligingly changed the zoning definition of family to include as many as five unrelated adults. As a private citizen I opposed that change in zoning, and voiced my opposition to every official I met.

Early in my administration, at my request the council reduced the definition from five to three unrelated adults. That solved part of the problem, but did nothing about multiple family housing zoning in single family neighborhoods. What if developers actually built at the highest density allowed? How might that affect parking and traffic? And what about the neighbors who had thought they were protected by zoning? Bloomington had a master plan to shape municipal growth, a plan more curse than blessing. Last modified in 1973, it was both outdated and deeply flawed at birth. The consequences, long delayed, came with a bang in my administration. Residents complained about the apartment invasion of single-family neighborhoods. A dense thicket of student housing across from I.U. Stadium caused constant conflict among neighbors, landlords, students and police. Traffic often jammed roads near the east side mall. We had to service new suburban subdivisions that the old plan had permitted with little forethought about service. I was determined to rectify the plan that had worked so poorly.

Many of these headaches came from planning decisions in the Hooker administration, when large tracts of land were zoned multifamily and commercial without regard to traffic congestion. Large tracts, zoned for high density, lay dormant and forgotten until developed years later, to the sudden dismay of neighbors. Now developers wanted more of the same, but times had changed. Somehow we had to do better. Others had tried. In 1989 the Bloomington Plan Commission, pressed for commercial development on the southeast side, tried to update sections of the old plan. After facing so many conflicting requests, the commission pretty much gave up.

It is hard to reverse a zoning decision, however bad. One peril is what lawyers call a "taking," an act that reduces the value of a property. The best way to make changes the community favored was to create a citywide master plan to supersede the old one. (A measure of our success was the minimal number of law suits our master plan engendered.) Bloomingtonians definitely wanted to protect the older neighborhoods, limit commercial east-side growth to traffic the city could handle, and stop sprawl on the outskirts.

It was not enough to protect neighborhoods. In addition, we had to produce guidelines for future growth. Pressures for urban sprawl were enormous. Developers made their profits on the appreciation of property *after* it was developed, so they were always looking for cheap land with future access to city services.

City government had broader interests. To protect the taxpayer we sought compact urban growth where city services were already at hand, as it is hugely expensive to upgrade roads and extend other city services. Most commercial and residential growth had been on the east side. Existing roads could handle no further growth in that direction, and upgrades were expensive. That is why we designed our master plan to re-direct some residential growth; to fill in the undeveloped land west of Rogers/Rockport Road and north of Tapp Road; and to foster some commercial growth on the westside.

THE TASK BEGINS

We knew this formidable task was more than our staff could handle, because rapid city growth had already overburdened the planning department. The additional work to produce a new master plan would push the department too hard. We took our first big step in the spring of 1990, when we called for bids and hired Camiros, a Chicago planning firm, to help our staff devise a plan in concert with the Bloomington Plan Commission. The place Camiros stepped into was a university community of 35,000 students and 7,000 faculty and staff; a town of 65,000; and a county, named for James Monroe, of 108,000.

As we wanted the new plan to reflect the views of the community, we picked two thousand households at random and mailed each one a survey with one hundred seven questions. The six hundred returns (thirty percent) provided a trustworthy cross section of opinion.

The respondents did not want to curtail development, residential or commercial. However, they worried about southeast development in the College Mall area, and they wanted local government to regulate developers more strictly. They were not sure where they wanted future commercial development. They recognized Bloomington's role as a regional service center, but wanted no more fast food restaurants. The necessary roads should be in place before any commercial development, and the developers should pay for those roads. They wanted to preserve the city's small-town charm, through careful design and landscaping of developments. They thought Bloomington had high environmental quality, but expected worse five years hence.

Bloomington Plan Director Tim Mueller announced a town meeting to review the survey. He encouraged all to attend, as did the newspaper. The four-hour meeting was on a Saturday morning, in a high school auditorium. The first of many similar meetings, it featured an overview of the master plan process, presentations by Camiros consultants, accounts of neighborhood concerns based on community meetings, and structured discussions chaired by Camiros representatives.[1]

About 250 attended that first meeting at BHS-South. They wanted to talk about multifamily housing in single-family neighborhoods. They thought it would be all right to have mid-rise buildings in the downtown as a way to strengthen commerce there. They wanted steps to preserve a vibrant, healthy downtown as an integral part of small town ambience. A convention center would be good. They liked the notion of small neighborhood shopping centers accessible to pedestrians or public transit. They generally approved Bloomington's role as a regional center, but some accepted the role with reluctance. And some, of course, thought the survey could have asked better questions.[2]

By mid-July two more public meetings had taken place, and Camiros representatives had met with business leaders over breakfast. Citizens who were uneasy with general scenarios began to demand more planning details. Camiros' Charles Neale, head of the Bloomington project, expressed surprise at the high level of public interest and participation. The unspoken sentiment was that if the public had kept quiet, Camiros could have turned to details more quickly. I cared little about speed; I wanted maximum public involvement.[3]

Soon Plan Director Tim Mueller announced that the plan commission would hold four public forums in August. These evening forums, in City Council Chambers from 7-10 p.m., would have less structure than the public meetings and spark freer comment on planning and zoning issues of greatest community concern. The August 2 forum would feature a briefing by Camiros and an open comment session. The August 8 forum would deal with growth management, traffic, development regulations, capital improvements and community character. August 15 would cover commercial development and the downtown, August 20 environmental quality and the protection of natural areas.

Meanwhile, Camiros and the city's planning staff would analyze three months' worth of research and discussion to lay the foundation for master plan policy. Mueller hoped to have a rough draft of the policy statement by September.[4]

Mueller was overoptimistic. September came and went with no sign of a draft. Camiros had never seen a more talkative town. Some thought we had coalesced into two factions, the residents of old neighborhoods and the environmentalists in one, and the developers in the other. They thought so despite the Camiros consultants' insistence that they had seen no antidevelopment sentiment in the community at large. Some thought the new plan would force major changes, some no change at all. But in the absence of a draft, such predictions had little purchase. For what it was worth, I was on record against any new commercial development in the College Mall area, and for maintaining the integrity of older residential areas.

Summer ended, but the talk went on. We staged several "congresses" to gain still more "community input" on the incipient master plan. Delegates to each congress were chosen by various organizations and special interest groups, from developers to neighborhood associations. Congress meetings were open to members of the public, who were supposed to look and listen but not comment. In the first one, September 25, about thirty delegates dealt with the environment, green space and parks. They had so much to talk about, the agenda spilled over into a second congress on October 9. The congresses ran through October, and ranged widely: Commercial development and downtown; the southeast sector; the older core neighborhoods; traffic and transportation; and the north and east sectors. Some met at City Council Chambers, others at the Older American Center on Walnut, and the Tourist and Convention Center. They started variously between 5:00 and 6:00 p.m., and two of them ran concurrently. Planning in October was intense.[5]

THE PLAN UNVEILED

The proposed new master plan made its debut on a Friday evening in the county library auditorium, the first day of the following March. Broadcast live on TV, the presentation combined a slide show with an explanation of the plan. Tim Mueller announced that copies of the 101-page document would be on view at the library and the Plan Department office, and could be had for the price of duplication. Accompanying maps and other visual aids would help to explain the plan's implications for each area of the city. The Plan Commission would chair four evening hearings in March and April to give residents a chance to say what they thought of the proposed plan, which would go to the commission for adoption on April 15.[6]

There was plenty of reaction.

Rosalie Roush, treasurer of the Elm Heights Neighborhood Association, presented a petition signed by 850 residents. They supported adoption of the plan, and opposed any significant changes to it.

Some objected to a proposed four-lane highway on Fifth Street. (Residents were right to speak up about this. The city had never supported this purely Camiros proposal, which died quietly.) Others emphasized the need for enforcement, lest the plan gather dust on some shelf.

Natasha Jacobs, running for mayor, was critical of the plan's omission of county schools and I.U. (although the city controls neither).[7]

A citizens group recently formed to provide feedback about city planning, Quality Growth, Inc., checked in. Paul Schneller disliked the plan's lack of long-range vision. Richard Martin thought the plan should reflect the public's desire that the city be known as a regional cultural center, not a regional shopping center. The group complimented the plan for its attention to mass transit, pedestrian and bicycle paths, and affordable housing.[8]

Many liked its concern for the protection of core neighborhoods. Chris Sturbaum thought the plan's provisions would have greatly helped his own revived neighborhood, Prospect Hill, had it been in effect earlier. Tim Mueller listed some of the protective provisions: creation of historic districts; investments in infrastructure; redevelopment of blighted and non-conforming buildings; enforcement of housing codes and traffic regulations; implementation of design review process; and limited conversion of residential properties to nonresidential uses.

Mueller also mentioned that the plan would arrest a neighborhood's decline into rental slumhood. It would do so by limiting the number of adult occupants in single-family dwellings. It would also limit the conversion of single-family into multifamily dwellings. These were defensive measures against predatory investors who would rent older homes at high rates to five or six young adults who could easily afford, say, four hundred dollars each. This lucrative practice would price young families out of the neighborhood market. And it would often bring radical change to a neighborhood's character in the form of more noise, rapid deterioration, and less attention to maintenance. The plan addressed neighborhood parking problems. For example, residential parking permits would make it easier to find a parking place near one's own home.[9]

Attorney Lynn Coyne, who represented College Mall management, disliked the restriction on College Mall development. He believed the plan should allow high quality commercial development. Tim Mueller disagreed. He thought the new plan would foster development throughout the rest of the community, and thus require less driving for access to services.

Developer Eric Stolberg acknowledged that a north side grocery store could spare shoppers a trip to the southeast side of town. However, College Mall development should not be ignored, and the southeast would continue to attract residential development. Mueller responded: The plan would redirect residential growth to the near west side.

Many developers framed such redirection as bad planning, an effort to force builders and buyers away from where they wanted to go. Ben Beard, of the Building Association of South Central Indiana, said builders worried about the master plan's restriction of growth. It restricted builders unfairly because, he said, "It would shut down as much as 85% of the marketplace." He added that developers, who are both businessmen and residents desirous of a beautiful city, still question whether city government could force citizens to live where they don't want to.[10]

The editorial opinion of the *Herald-Times*, presented on my birthday, was succinct: "Master plan good, not perfect." The editors liked the the plan's protection of older core neighborhoods and affordable single-family homes; continued development of the downtown; environmental protection; and redirection of development to the west side. They dismissed as unrealistic the prospect of reducing traffic congestion by means of pedestrian paths, bicycle trails and enhanced (public) transit. (Note: All three of those prospects have come to pass. And they have reduced, but not eliminated, traffic congestion.) They disliked the restriction on further commercial development in the College Mall area. They predicted more traffic congestion from further residential development in the southeast. As for the plan's general philosophy of commercial development, they thought it contrary to the free enterprise system. Still and all, the plan had involved much time, much effort, and much input from residents. It provided ". . . a good framework for Bloomington's future."[11]

THE PLAN APPROVED

On April 15 the Bloomington Plan Commission, in a packed meeting room in the Municipal Building, approved the proposed master plan. The unanimous vote came after a long parade of citizens who spoke for or against the proposal. Commission chairman Tom Swafford said, "It has not been easy, and it has not been fun. I have had (Camiros consultant Charles Neale) tell me that he has never seen a community that wanted to talk so much about so many things."[12]

The final step of the approval process came on May 15, in another packed room, when the Bloomington City Council approved the plan, without amendment, by a vote of 8-1. Republican Steve Hogan cast the dissenting vote.

Before the vote Hogan presented an amendment, in behalf of businessman Richard Rechter, to allow further commercial development in the College Mall area. Rechter warned that the proposed plan was a no-growth policy that would hurt the community. The council rejected the amendment. However, it approved a motion from Democrat Jim Regester in behalf of the Bloomington Chamber of Commerce. The motion would incorporate nine statements into the plan, not to change it, but to emphasize particular elements.

The council declared that their approval of policy had not created a working plan. The crucial next step was to embody the policy in zoning regulations that would put the new master plan to work. The plan commission would formulate these zoning regulations for approval by the council. Community groups and individuals should stay involved, and make sure the regulations truly embodied the intent of the plan and its creators.[13]

THE PLAN APPLIED

The summer passed with little ado about planning. The calm ended on August 26, when the Wininger-Stolberg Group proposed a north side shopping center at Kinser Pike and the bypass. The Bloomington Plan Commission had rejected such proposals before, but the new plan seemed to support it. Nevertheless, the commission voted 6-4 against. Now it would go to the city council for a final decision.

Why did the commission reject the proposal, when the plan supported the siting there of a neighborhood shopping center? The reason given was that the project seemed intended more as a regional draw than a neighborhood center. Its fatal detail was a sit-down restaurant proposed for the seven-acre site. Some saw that as an "out lot," a feature specifically forbidden by the plan.

The commission conceded that the decision had been difficult. It was witnessed by a crowd of citizens who spilled out of the City Council Chambers and into the corridors of the Municipal Building. Some lived in the affected area; more than 600 had signed a petition against the project. Some thought they were already served by a neighborhood grocery and pharmacy; a 60,000-foot shopping center would add too much traffic to their already overburdened neighborhood. Some worried that the extra traffic would endanger children of the nearby elementary school.[14]

Another tremor came at 3 a.m. Thursday, September 12, when the Bloomington City Council gave its preliminary approval to the very project the Plan Commission had rejected. The vote was decisive, 7-1, with one abstention. The final decision was scheduled for the following week.

Councilman John Fernandez, the sole dissenter, was not happy with his colleagues' view of the freestanding out lot. This out lot would be restricted to one of four possible uses: video rental/sales, a branch bank, a business/professional office, or a sit-down restaurant. The abstainer, Iris Kiesling, wanted further clarification of what constituted a neighborhood shopping center and out lot. Fernandez responded, "I don't think you could get it any clearer—the master plan says 'no out lots.' I can't understand how my colleagues can totally ignore that language."

Resident Mike Bailey had his own reasons to be unhappy with the council. Fellow residents had talked all night about traffic and safety issues, only to be told that they should have been party to the process that created the master plan. He had learned his lesson. Henceforth he would pay less attention to national elections, and more attention to local politicians and their positions on local issues.

Pam Service made a councilwoman's lament. You weigh all the options, and do what you think is right. "And in the end, someone is always mad at you and you have made enemies."[15]

City Council Chambers were packed again the following week. Again the discussion ran from the evening into the early morning hours, with much public comment back and forth. The overflow crowd sat on the floor, stood against walls, and filled the hallway, where they could watch the proceedings on the cable television monitor.

They were treated to some lawyering by Ted Najam for the neighborhood, and Bill Finch for the developers. Najam called it the only site in the master plan where an out lot was not permitted. To approve the project would violate neighborhood trust, set a dangerous precedent, and violate the English language: "no out lot" would henceforth mean "yes, out lot." He threw in the hazards of additional traffic, spoilage of scenery, and environmental problems.

Finch called the project exactly what the plan envisioned. "Neither the store nor the project is a mega-anything, except a mega brouhaha for some people in the community who don't want any development in that area at all." He called it the most under served part of town, with twenty-three percent of the population but only seven percent of the area for grocery shopping.

This time the vote was 7-2, with Fernandez and Kiesling against. Perhaps Councilman Lloyd Olcott captured the majority sentiment, "We've got to grow. We're a major regional center. If you really want no development, you ought to move to Paoli."[16]

I announced my hiring of a code enforcement manager, Pat Bookwalter, for the new Growth Policies Plan. She brought much experience in city redevelopment, parks and recreation, and housing code departments. It would be her job to monitor site plan compliance in new development; to implement new environmental legislation; create new, improved procedures to track and monitor municipal code; and guide various codes—housing, site plan, building, zoning, nuisance and others—into compliance with the new master plan codes. I went on to announce progress on ordinances about resident parking, erosion control, and revision of the zoning ordinance.[17]

Two days later, this pleasant news sank like a stone when I vetoed the council's approval of the north side shopping center. How did I justify my first and only veto? To approve that freestanding out lot would get the new plan off on the wrong foot. Approval would violate clear guidelines, erode public confidence, and diminish a core city neighborhood. My veto reflected not a no-growth policy, but a pro-plan policy. If it chose to do so, the council could override me by a 6-3 vote (the original was 7-2).

Fernandez applauded my decision. Service said she would reconsider her favorable vote on the proposed development. Others said they would stand by their original votes as the best thing for the community. A few among the council accused me of bowing to popular pressure. Bill Finch, former McCloskey staffer and the attorney for Wininger-Stolberg, implied that I might be a fool or a knave. He said I might not have vetoed the project had I sat through the hours of debate that other officials had endured. He thought I had made "a real mistake" on an issue that went to "the fundamental principle of the master plan . . . . And if the veto is being used to pull votes in the November election, that is an even worse decision. This is too important an issue to be politicized and I certainly hope no one does that." Heaven forbid.[18]

At the next council meeting Republican Marilyn House took the high road. "Appeals based on political and emotional reasons shouldn't be allowed to direct our vote." Democrat Service changed her previous vote, and supported the veto so as to reaffirm public confidence in the new master plan. "This is our first chance to implement the master plan and I wish we had a better test case to do it with."

The sometimes emotional debate drew another overflow audience. These veterans of marathon discussion were worn down; they applauded Republican Kirk White's suggestion, a 90-minute limit. No doubt they had heard the same points before. Attorney Bill Finch thought the out lot was only a handy smokescreen to defeat the project. Opposing counsel Ted Najam disagreed: The plan prohibited an out lot, and "no" meant "no." Two site owners were ill, but sent their niece with a message that said they had minded their land as responsible stewards long enough, and wanted to develop it now as the master plan permitted. Another resident thought the development would produce more "mall sprawl" without reducing crosstown traffic or conferring any other civic benefit. He wanted to wait until after the next election so a new council could make the decision. Several weary council members smiled in agreement. Republican Lloyd Olcott, not up for reelection, said zoning debates would always generate controversy, with or without a master plan. Clever attorneys would have a field day as they used the plan to support or oppose a position. Democrat Jim Regester had visited the site three times that day as he tried to visualize the projected change. Republican Steve Hogan thought the veto was a ploy to gather votes. Moreover, the strong no-growth sentiment in the community was the fault of the present administration and the previous one (both Democratic). And where was the necessary infrastructure? It is slow in coming, replied Democrat Iris Kiesling. "We can't always have what we want when we want it."

By a vote of 6-3 the council overrode my veto, and approved the project.

Council President Fernandez hoped the vote would not be seen as the demise of the master plan. The plan, he said, served an important function as it narrowed the debate in its first test case. It was alive, he said, and well.[19]

OF POLITICS AND PLANNING

Days before the election the master plan popped up as a big election issue. Tom Swafford, plan commission chairman, served a big helping of understatement: If the next mayor doesn't support the plan, we will have wasted a lot of time and tax money.

The three mayoral candidates unlimbered their oars. I had heard Republican Balint Vazsonyi call the plan "a dangerous instrument." I mentioned that some of his biggest contributors were developers.

Vazsonyi replied. His second biggest contribution had come through a professional cellist with no interest in buying, selling, or building. He chose not to estimate the size of his substantial war chest, but thought it proof of support for him, and opposition to the Allison administration. His own polls showed the PCB incinerator as the biggest issue, followed by jobs, roads and traffic.

My response came through Mike Davis, my Deputy Mayor, as I was in Washington talking culture and economic development with Pacific Rim ambassadors. Our door-to-door discussions during the campaign revealed the master plan as the key election issue, said Davis. He added that the plan could be derailed if the mayor were not reelected.

Independent candidate Ron Smith did not oppose all development. Yes, College Mall was a problem. However, it was not fair for the Democrats to call a press conference just to blast Richard Rechter's proposal. It was rude. It reflected prejudice against Rechter rather than the proposal.

The 112-acre Rogers Farm was a scenic piece of land southeast of the College Mall. Rechter wanted to build a strip mall on thirty-five acres, plus mixed residential development on the rest. The land in question was zoned for single-family residential development, plus some low density multifamily units. It was not zoned commercial.

Republican Steve Hogan agreed with Smith. No one should attack a proposal before it has started through the system. Fernandez disagreed. He called the proposal such a blatant deviation from the master plan, presented so near the election, that the community should be made aware of it now. And so it was.[20]

The planning issue infected the at-large city council races. Republican candidate Patricia Jeffries said the plan had not worked. It had become a tool of confrontation, not cooperation. It had been too much designed by Chicago consultants unfamiliar with Bloomington's problems. Democratic candidates praised the plan.[21]

The election results returned me to office with a big Democratic majority on the city council, 8-1.

Soon after the election the Bloomington Plan Commission took up Rechter's strip mall proposal, and turned it down with one dissenting vote. They said the rezoning request went against a major tenet of the new master plan, to restrict growth in the College Mall area.

The dissenter, Rod Young, criticized the plan as elitist. He liked the idea of financing infrastructure improvements from property tax increases proceeding from the project.

Rechter said he would appeal his rejected proposal to the city council in December. He wanted me to tell the community about the four hundred jobs and the $5.8 million payroll the town would forgo if his project were denied.

Audience member William Edgerton had some choice comments for the commission. "The profit motive and the sex drive are two powerful forces." But Rechter, he said, instead of trying to get the most for his money, could better use his thirty-five acres as a city park, and enter "Bloomington history as one of the city's greatest benefactors. Then he could develop the other seventy-seven acres into a profitable and attractive residential area." Resident Merle Englander said the new master plan should not be violated for the sake of money. "One of the missing things here is what is really good for the people. We live here because of the kind of community this is and has been."[22]

The council took up Rechter's proposal on December 11 for a preliminary vote. The paper had already reported, correctly, that if the council approved the proposal, I would veto it.

Republican Council member Marilyn House, who had lost in the November election, said that her east side constituents had made it clear as she went door-to-door that they opposed this kind of development. She would vote against the Rechter proposal.

Rechter reminded the council of those six hundred additional jobs (originally reported as four hundred), and the additional revenues the city could use for infrastructure improvements "without costing the community." But two and a half hours of public comment were dominated by audience members who stepped up to the podium and talked of the project's high cost to the community. It would put more traffic on already overburdened roads. Any new jobs created would be minimum wage jobs. The competition from new stores might shut down similar stores already here.

The vote was 8-1 against, with Hogan the only dissenter.[23]

The final vote came a week later. House repeated the reason she would vote against the proposal. Kirk White, the only Republican who had kept his seat, thought it might be a mistake to reject the proposal, the likes of which many communities would welcome. However, as this community plainly wanted no such development, he felt compelled to vote against. City Planning Director Tim Mueller commented that the housing part of the plan was reasonable, but the commercial development would subvert the master plan's goal of containing commercial growth in the southeast.

On the other side, Council member Steve Hogan said the community needed more shopping choices, without which shoppers would go elsewhere. It was commendable that the city push commercial development to the west side, but it would simply not happen. "Retailers have had an opportunity for years to go out on the west side and they don't choose to." (Note: In a very few years Bloomingtonians would find both a Wal-Mart and a Sam's Club "out on the west side.")

In response to objections, Rechter proposed changes. He would remove some possible businesses, such as bars and manufacturers. He would reduce the commercial acreage from 35 to 30. He replaced his original strip mall with a drawn plan for a building complex with landscaping and parking areas.

Representatives of east-side neighborhood groups stepped up and repeated their objections, including traffic problems, low-paid jobs, destructive business competition.

Again the council voted 8-1 against, with Hogan the only dissenter.

Rechter was not sure about future plans for the area, but knew what he thought about the council. "We've got a very, very liberal government. They're antigrowth, antibusiness, and they're going to turn out to be anti the average person, in my opinion. But we're going to have to let that cycle happen."[24]

I appreciated developers' consuming interest in local politics. A mere rezoning could mean a ton of money in their pockets. In contrast with neighborhoods, which became active occasionally, say when a development threatened their particular location, developers had a continuing interest, year in and year out, that they defended without cease. Their defense often embodied generous campaign contributions to politicians who seemed to favor their cause.

I tried to treat developers fairly, but my first duty was to the general welfare. However, there could be no doubt about the emotions evoked by anything to do with planning or zoning. At one point in our work on the new growth policy plan I arrived at my office to find that a box of flowers had been delivered to me. The box was three or four feet long. Inside were a dozen roses, black roses, each one withered, dry and dead.

Someone had cared enough to send the very worst. We all agreed that this extravagant gesture must have had something to do with planning and zoning.

MAKING IT WORK OR NOT

As the year began the *Herald-Times* wished for "A reasoned and balanced application of Bloomington's master plan to proposals for future development, especially in the southeast side." It had high praise for the new intersection of College Mall and Sare Road with Moores Pike.[25]

The next proposal dispelled any notion that two precedents, Wininger-Stolberg and Rechter, would make application any easier. Tim Henke wanted to build five duplexes and four single-family homes where the plan said he could not. Accordingly, he asked the city to change a residential single-family zone into a planned unit development zone. Area residents and city council members were divided at the preliminary hearing.[26] A week later the council approved Henke's request, 8-1, as an improvement to the area. This came after a three-hour discussion of the pros and cons. Many residents were unhappy with the proposal. They thought, reasonably enough, that it would change their neighborhood from residential to rental, contrary to the master plan.[27]

There was no letup. Terry Elkins laid a proposal before the Plan Commission. He wanted to build a twenty-four-unit condominium in a place zoned single-family residential, where only sixteen housing units were allowed, and no apartments. To no one's surprise, his proposal drew criticism from neighborhood residents and commission members.[28, 29]

At this point it was good indeed to learn that the outside world knew and appreciated our labors in city planning. In February I went to Minneapolis for a mayors' conference on city design; Bloomington had been invited for our exemplary effort in coping with growth. Of special interest was our initiative in creating the new Growth Policies Plan (the "master plan"). In meetings with city designers and scholars I talked mainly about our new Showers project and west side renovations.[30]

In the meantime, the city moved ahead with regulations to implement the master plan. Losing no chance to engage neighborhood residents in the planning and zoning process, we handed out maps and asked small groups to sketch how they wanted their neighborhoods to look in ten years.[31]

Our planning department staged public forums on possible changes in zoning ordinances. There was a memorable night meeting in a high school auditorium, a gathering of hundreds of the restive and the unruly. Developers and landlords approached the microphone to voice anxiety, fear, and a strong desire to be heard in full before any final decisions. They were angry. I stood up to assure them that there was no rush, we would take all the time we needed, we would hear all of their concerns. They applauded and calmed down. We canceled the remaining forums until we could make the rezoning more palatable.

To refine our proposal I asked our planning staff to draw several discussion groups from different geographic areas. Each group comprised representatives of neighborhood organizations, landlord associations, banking, and other diverse interests. Their purpose was to work out differences. The new proposal would strive to preserve community character and the value of existing property, and we would make the necessary changes before the Plan Commission resumed its rezoning. We insisted that the delay was not a retreat from the new master plan, and commission member Jack Hopkins concurred: "This should not by anyone be interpreted as a step back from the Growth Policies Plan."[32]

Meanwhile, the world's biggest merchandiser stood poised to endorse the master plan in deed, if not in word. In May Wal-Mart asked the Plan Commission to change the outline plan for a piece of land on the southwest side, zoned commercial, near Bloomfield Road and the Indiana 37 Bypass. If all went well, the company would build a Wal-Mart Store and a Sam's Club at the site, over 250,000 square feet of new retail space.

Tim Mueller recalled a common objection to the master plan. The plan could not influence the market; if retailers wanted to go east, it could not head them west. He said this retailer probably would have preferred to go east, but headed west in accordance with the plan. The promised benefits were about to materialize. Indiana 37 would give easy access to new commercial development, and spare College Mall from further traffic congestion.[33] The basic proposal received final approval a few months later, and the result now stands on the southwest side of town.

THE ALL-IMPORTANT MATTER OF PARKING

Among long time residents, few things mattered more than parking—especially if they had no place to park but the street. Life held few greater irritants than to lose a race with some stranger for the parking space right in front of one's own house.

Later that month, after a year's worth of overhaul and fine tuning the neighborhood parking proposal made it past the Bloomington City Council. It would take effect come summer, August 15. Parking stickers would cost neighborhood residents ten dollars per year to park on city streets south of the university, weekdays from 8 a.m. to 5 p.m. Neighborhood residents could buy one visitor permit per household. Special parking provisions were made for nonresident property owners, and for residents expecting more visitors than the permits allowed.

Every three months the parking plan would be evaluated during a one-year trial period. It could be changed or canceled in any quarter. Under a sunset provision the ordinance would expire on August 15, 1993, unless extended by the council.

Parking without a permit would incur a flat ten-dollar fine; the fine for a sticker on an ineligible auto would be twenty dollars. Fines and permit sales would support the program, and any extra money would go into an Alternative Transportation Fund toward reducing our dependence on autos.[34]

THE BACK STRETCH

In June I formed a citizens advisory committee as a sounding board for implementation policies, such as the downzoning proposal that had heated up that high school auditorium. Depending on whom you asked, my advisory committee was a "great idea" or "bound to fail," and "broadly representative" or "under the mayor's thumb."[35]

In the summer of 1993, over a year after the famous meeting in the school auditorium, we were ready to unveil a revised rezoning proposal. Time would tell if it would polarize the community again. It had withstood inspection by a citizens' advisory committee, but how would it strike the public? Tim Mueller reminded the press that the thirty-five-page document was only an outline, ready for presentation but not for a hearing. The hearings would come later, along with zoning details. Camiros consultants would make the presentation.

Mueller recalled the six primary goals.

> Protect older core neighborhoods.
> Continue downtown development.
> Protect the environment.
> Restrict east side development.
> Redirect development to the west side.
> Mitigate traffic by means of pedestrian paths, bicycle trails and public transit.

We kept harping on the welfare of older neighborhoods as irreplaceable resources. On the same note, if we meant to preserve residential character we had to stop making single-family houses into multi-family ones.[36] Many found it hard to understand why this issue aroused such intense feelings, but landlords and bankers understood. Landlords foresaw a sharp decline in rental revenue. Bankers foresaw trouble from landlord debtors faced with high mortgage payments. Some shouted their fears to the world, on roadside billboards on the way into town that urged viewers to protect their property against Tomi Allison and Tim Mueller.

When the commissioners saw the new plan they sat up and noted the number and variety of zoning districts, twenty or more. For example, its different residential zones provided single-family homes with various zoning densities, ranging from one house per 2.5 acre lot up to seven houses per acre. It showed multifamily zones with housing densities from seven to 15 units per acre. Various commercial districts ranged from limited development to shopping centers, industrial districts from light to heavy zones. Special districts with unique zones included Indiana University, Bloomington Hospital and certain quarries. Special overlays signified places, such as lake watersheds, with extra requirements for those who would build there. We had it all.

The next steps toward a zoning ordinance would be public hearings and commissioners' suggestions, then back to Camiros for first draft preparation. Commissioners, if their comments were any clue, might want to examine the size of the signs in Bloomington (too big), architectural and landscaping standards, and parking lot sizes.[37]

Early the following year the public rained complaints on the Plan Commission at a meeting billed as the master plan's first audit. Someone from Monroe County Housing Solutions thought new zoning policies had raised housing costs and cut the supply of affordable housing. A resident called the zoning a "political payoff to a handful of residents who don't want to tolerate students after 5 p.m." Business types bemoaned the scarcity of cheap land zoned for industry and commerce. Someone thought the plan would cause urban flight. Builders thought it hard or impossible to achieve compact urban form because they first had to petition for zoning variances. Another complained that it was not enough to have a forum where residents could air their complaints; they needed objective measures of how the plan was meeting its goals. It had been another "can't do" meeting.

The commissioners listened. They said they would use public comments even as the map and the new zoning ordinance took shape.[38]

A few weeks later a quake rattled the town when the planners spoke of a lofty condominium that might disrupt the city skyline. Its developer was Bill Cook's CFC Inc. It would be eleven stories high, the biggest residential building in town. It would become a center of attention at 500 North Walnut.

The quorum of commissioners who happened to attend the meeting liked the proposal. So did a big majority of the small public crowd in attendance. What with other houses that would have to make way for the twenty-one-unit structure, the net gain would be only fifteen housing units. Critics might think this kind of housing too rich for local blood, but others looked forward to such residency. CFC attorney Bill Finch thought a low-end unit might cost around $150,000.

To build up, rather than out, certainly seemed consistent with master plan goals, but Tim Mueller feared the building might be too tall. Finch disagreed, and cited certain tall buildings on the I.U. campus. Mueller thought the verdicts of both officialdom and the public might come down to esthetics. Commissioner Tom Swafford thought the building not "bad-looking," but worried about the shadow it might cast on the neighborhood. Finch assured him that CFC had a shadow impact study under way. The commissioners scheduled a second hearing.[39]

When the second hearing rolled around, the vocal part of the public was not so sympathetic as before. Several approved of the project, but thought the proposed building had the wrong style (Gothic) and height (165 feet) for the surrounding neighborhood. (First called a twenty-one-unit structure, its reported size had grown to twenty-seven units.) City Council member Patricia Cole thought it looked more like a church than a residence, and spoke right up: "I don't like the design." She thought the city needed a design review board; the one provided by the new master plan was not yet in place.

Bill Finch, for CFC, showed how the building's winter shadow would cover three city blocks. John Wood, owner of a rental business next door, had his own way of putting it; after 2 p.m. the shadow would keep all sunlight from his workplace "for eternity."

In simulations, at a few blocks' distance the projected building looked about twice the height of its surrounding structures. Close up, said a resident, it would look monumental. But the commissioners fretted more about possible traffic problems than esthetics. They noticed that the building's underground garage was on a one-way street. This meant that a resident motorist heading north on Walnut would have to travel several blocks to arrive at the garage.

At last the commission approved Cook's plan, but only if the city would change at least part of Ninth Street into a two-way street, or make some equivalent arrangement. This recommendation would have to go to the Bloomington Traffic Commission before City Council could act.[40]

About a month later the paper described the proposal as a 177-foot limestone building, thirteen stories high, with twenty-three condominium units, two floors of utilities and mechanicals, and parking underground. The proposal was in deep trouble with City Council, which was deadlocked 4-4 in the absence of one member, Iris Kiesling. Now she was back in town, and the council would vote soon with all members present. She was not telling the press which way she would go. She was saying nice things about the Cook organization and what fine things it had done for the town. She was saying how we truly did need upscale housing downtown. The building did have a height problem. She supported the proposed tax abatement, worth about $1,245,000 over ten years, as a way for the community to support private investment. She would consider all the pros and cons.

She finally thought it was too much building on too little land. Council rejected the proposal, 5-4. Council tried to pave the way for a smaller project, but Bill Cook would have none of it. He had watched the disappointing outcome at home on television, and his project would not be back. His response was, "It is just pure and simple—you go through this once in a lifetime. It is not going to happen again. I don't want to take the heat." Cook thought emotion had played into the decision. "I have never based a decision on emotion and that is one of the things that hit here. Personal preference seemed to take priority over the logic of the building and the economics of the building." As for Gothic, wasn't it still going strong after 900 years?[41]

I had already warned the press that we were in for a long, hot summer of planning and zoning. I had set a deadline, September 21, for the adoption of maps and zoning ordinance for the new Growth Policies Plan. It would take much time, work and public participation, but we would have to finish the job this year.

We started in 1989, and adopted the plan in 1991. In the words of Rod Young, Plan Commission president, "It was a little bit more participatory than we thought to begin with." As we depended heavily on community feedback, we stood ready to add more public meetings if needed, but not to extend the deadline.

As the *Herald-Times* reported, business people and developers were speaking out. Doug Jones, of Positive Progress, Inc., explained my rush as a desire to finish the controversial part well before the following year's election. He thought the mayor's timetable was ill-timed and haphazard; looking toward the 1995 election, she would jeopardize the "public process and trust."

Nonsense. As council president Jim Sherman pointed out, the next step was not "something ground breaking and brand new. That in fact was done in 1991." The city was already functioning in accord with the master plan, even though all the zoning maps and rules were not yet in place.

Tim Mueller said he had broken the draft into three parts: procedure and process; basic zones and their requirements; and special zones. Copies of each part would soon go on sale at two commercial outlets.[42]

Thanks to Doug Jones and the right-wing press, the whole nation learned of Bloomington's impending death by master plan. Co-written by T. Craig Ladwig, vice president of the Indiana Policy Review Foundation, their nationally syndicated article claimed to document how the Bloomington "experiment" in land use policies, prescribed by "land-use progressives," had raised the cost of housing. It had done this by means of a "taking"—reducing the value of private property by regulatory fiat.

Tim Mueller took umbrage. What experiment? Our growth policy plan enjoyed great community participation and support from many sectors. In no way did it reflect an antigrowth mentality. We had tried to strike a reasonable balance between growth and preservation, as had many other "well planned progressive growing communities."

Jones and Ladwig knew better. Bloomington's "exclusionary zoning policies" did not so much manage growth, as deflect it "willy-nilly toward less wealthy neighbors." Moreover, the new zoning would probably create still more of the pollution, congestion and urban sprawl that the planners professed to oppose. Saddest of all was that those wrong-head planners might actually believe that they were doing the right thing. But surely no one failed to see the sinister intent: To protect "certain people's property at the expense of someone else." Ghetto Bloomington was on the way.

Land-use progressives indeed. Horrors![43]

Three months later the Greater Bloomington Chamber of Commerce took a position directly opposed to its bedfellow, the Indiana Policy Review. As the Chamber saw it, the plan was going to be too hard on the less fortunate members of our community.

I am not making this up. In November the Chamber's Master Plan Committee staged a public forum at the Convention Center attended by about sixty citizens. The committee warned that to adopt the ordinance as written would be to "force many workers employed in Monroe County to move to neighboring counties to live." Tim Henke, commenting on the plan's affordable housing policy, said that the ordinance would force people to drive to work in Bloomington. "We'll never build another boarding house and have little multifamily units or apartments." Committee member Steve Smith agreed. "I think that is already happening. We need to rectify that. I don't think there's any provision in the ordinance for affordable housing."

Part of the problem, Henke said, was that everything in the code discouraged small units. We should revise it so as to encourage the building of smaller units—efficiencies, one- and two-bedroom apartments—and multifamily housing. If the code would allow higher density and require fewer amenities, it would permit cheaper construction.[44]

AND INTO THE SUNSET

Herald-Times *cartoon, 1994, following my announcement that I would not seek another term as mayor. Original drawing presented to me by the artist, Dave Coverly.*

Two weeks later I announced that I would not run for another term as mayor.

In anticipation the *Herald-Times* wondered whether I was ready to retire. Why should she? The current term of "the 12-year veteran" had been pretty good. The master plan was nearly in place, and the Showers renovation was moving ahead. Nevertheless, just to be on the safe side the paper sniffed out Democratic and Republican hopefuls.

Former Democratic city councilman John Fernandez said that any Democrat would have to offer voters a new vision. He himself was an unlikely candidate. (He became both a candidate and my successor.)

State Rep. Mark Kruzan, D-Bloomington, had expressed interest, but with his recent appointment as House minority whip was now less likely to pursue the mayorship. He chose not to discuss his plans. (He succeeded Fernandez as mayor.) The *Herald-Times* mentioned five other Democrats.

Kirk White, the lone Republican city councilman, expected that my departure would produce "quite a primary." He thought I had done a good job, but detected "a sense of urgency about change." Ready for a new challenge, one option for him was "to continue serving the city as its chief operating officer," by which he meant "mayor." Republican John Smith, county councilman and party chairman, called my administration arrogant and antibusiness. Many had talked to him about running, and he was giving it strong consideration.[45]

On its editorial page the *Herald-Times* trotted out its faint-praise specialist. Successes notwithstanding, she was right not to run again. The decision was good news. Not that she had been a bad mayor; she had not. It was simply time for a change, and new ideas.

Oh, the newspaper allowed, the list was impressive enough. Two new fire stations, three new parks, the old ones renovated. New social service programs, such as Kid City. Infrastructure improvements throughout. Better relations with I.U. A community recycling program. Two parking garages, and a lot of beautification. A "crowning achievement" was downtown revitalization through public-private cooperation, an Allison trademark. The Showers renovation, a new hotel.

The historians, said the paper, would have the final word on the Growth Policies Plan. In the meantime, some citizens thought it the best possible thing for Bloomington, others the worst. It would need strong leadership, and some depolarization.

Maybe the council didn't deserve its no-growth label, but it had certainly earned its inhospitable-to-business reputation—not entirely her fault, but she is mayor after all. And what about those PCBs? We know, they reared their ugly heads nearly eight years before she became mayor. But look at the millions the city has spent on the problem, and the PCBs are still there! At least nobody built an incinerator on her watch.

She had been a tireless, problem-solving, consensus-building facilitator, all right—cause after cause, day after day. How she must have loved those committees and those task forces!

Her standard would be hard to equal, but it was time for her to let someone try.[46]

Our September 21 deadline passed, but right after Christmas we presented our final revision of the proposed zoning ordinances. Better yet, we presented it along with a comparison copy that showed changes from the September 19 version. Public hearings on the 192-page ordinance would begin January 17.

The ordinance was the culmination of many public meetings among city planners, plan commissioners, city council, neighborhood associations, and the Chamber of Commerce Master Plan Committee. The thing had zoning maps, land use regulations, and procedures for implementation of rules. You could buy a copy at either of two commercial outlets, or see one at the Municipal Building, the Monroe County Public Library, or the I.U. Library.[47]

In late January, 1995, I gave my final State of the City Address, "A Climate of Success." It was an upbeat message with a recitation of achievements of which all Bloomingtonians—citizens, volunteers, and civil servants alike—could be proud. As usual, I kept it short and simple. I thought it went well; even the *Herald-Times* editors were complimentary, aside from a little whining about the climate for business and developers.[48]

In April—seven months late, and four years after passage of the Growth Policies Plan—city council passed the zoning ordinance to implement the plan. Council imposed a now familiar preference for shorter buildings, no taller than eighty feet downtown, or forty feet along Kirkwood from Indiana to the square. The proposed ordinance would have allowed some downtown buildings to sprout as high as 120 feet.

We had worked with citizens, businesspersons and developers, and they had listened to one another. There was widespread satisfaction with the final product, but not universal. Some said we had toned down our emphasis on single-family housing. For example, in single-family zones several multifamily rentals were "grandfathered" in as islands of multifamily residences. Some said our watersheds needed more environmental controls. Some thought we needed more protection of trees and green space, more attention to traffic mitigation.

Perhaps they were right. We had said repeatedly that the plan and the zoning ordinance were meant as living documents, subject to change—we hoped for the better—in light of experience. It was time for us, but never the town, to cry, "Done!" with planning and zoning.[49, 50]

BUT FIRST . . .

We should have seen a warning in the May 21 headline: "Whitehall Crossing is on track. Strip mall for west side may bring upscale megastores, cinema." A developer hoped to begin construction in autumn of a "huge shopping center at the northwest corner of Whitehall Pike and the Indiana 37 bypass west of Bloomington." The center, called Whitehall Crossing, would not be enclosed like College Mall, but rather a strip design, said an executive of Gates Development Corp. It would cover 600,000 square feet—the biggest thing on the west side, and only a tad smaller than College Mall. The developer hoped to attract several megastores that had not yet located in Bloomington, and a movie theater complex.

A current occupant, sign-maker Hall Signs, would move north to an industrial park. "If the commercial development is approved, about seventy acres of industrial land will be opened up for potential development to the west of the strip mall." If the commercial development is approved . . . .

Now, who would have to approve the commercial development? The Bloomington Plan Commission, followed by the Bloomington City Council. If you had been a member of the commission or the council, how would you have voted?

To understand the conflicting pressures of that time and place one must understand that the area in question lacked the commercial zoning necessary for the proposed Whitehall development, a commercial enterprise. It was zoned for light manufacturing because the community needed such space. It was well situated for light manufacturing, but not heavy commercial use, because of potential traffic jams on inadequate roads. Of course the developers were there, with their steady fixation on short term profits, but whence came the opposing pressures?

Some came from Monroe County Commissioners. In Indiana, if county government has no ordinance for planning and zoning, those matters are left to city government within a limited space outside the city—specifically, within the city's "two-mile fringe." The Whitehall proposal happened to come up when the county was moving to take over the zoning for the two-mile fringe. It also happened that the county favored the commercial zoning desired by the developer. A big carrot was his promise to extend a road through the rest of the land, zoned light manufacturing, all the way to Curry Pike, making the land more attractive to prospective new manufacturing plants.

Additional pressure came from citizens of the Highland Village Neighborhood Association. Many of them thought they had been underserved by commerce centered in malls on the distant east side of town. They thought the proposed commercial development would improve their lot by bringing more stores closer to their neighborhood.

Owners of a prized local business, Hall Signs, spoke up. Hall was ready to expand to a bigger site, but could not afford to move unless it could sell its present site as suitable for commercial development. Was there any way its present zoning could be changed from light manufacturing to commercial?

The Whitehall Crossing proposal sailed right through the Bloomington Plan Commission. The public made little outcry. It sailed through City Council, 6-1. Pam Service explained her lonely vote. "My feeling is the master plan zoned this land industrial for a purpose. This is prime industrial land and I just don't think it's appropriate to change it to commercial." She was reluctant to trade such a precious asset for the short-term gains of more shopping opportunities. There would be both economic gain and loss, and she was not sure how the two would balance out. We should remember, she said, that with every new store or restaurant, some existing business is affected.

Jim Tolen, president of Highland Village Neighborhood Association, was pleased. The west side was "hungry for developments like this."

So was the newspaper. "It was with great relief and pleasure that [the *Herald-Times*] saw the Bloomington City Council vote to approve zoning to permit the development of a giant new commercial development, Whitehall Crossing, on the city's west side." For accessibility there could hardly be a better location, and any future industry could always locate further west. The new mall could only strengthen the community economically, contrary to the grim protectors of the status quo. So a few marginal businesses go down. Such is the free market. Besides, mall-crawling is how the public prefers to shop. Isn't it fine how politicians behave in an election year, when they act in fear of public wrath?[51, 52, 53]

What the future actually held in store for this area was a mix of the good with the bad. Whitehall Crossing became an attractive development with complementary landscaping. Originally there was to be no cut to the bypass, on the well founded principle that a throughway should have no cuts. Somehow the cut materialized anyway. The area immediately to the west has not developed as light manufacturing as hoped, and has inspired some controversy. Subsequently the public witnessed a heated dispute between the county and the developer about who was supposed to maintain the western access road.

Some time later the area adjacent to Whitehall Crossing and further west developed as a commercial area in a hodgepodge of disconnected roads with no discernible planning.

The area south of Whitehall Pike, zoned light manufacturing, developed haphazardly after I left office. When the county took charge, the county definition of zoning allowed some commercial development in areas zoned for light manufacturing. The area quickly turned mostly commercial. We had tried to limit commercial growth where roads could not handle the traffic that such commerce would generate. Although some of those roads have been upgraded, travel there remains a horrendous drive. West side development has brought us more big box stores, but their arrival has forced out several local businesses. Some of the development is attractive, some is not. The west side deserved better.

I ask again, how would you have voted as a member of the Bloomington Plan Commission or the Bloomington City Council? Before you answer, give yourself some hindsight: Visit Whitehall Crossing, and take a good look around. Did you enjoy the drive? Do you like the appearance of the surrounding neighborhood? What do you think of the traffic patterns in the area? The merchandise? What do you think of the developer's prediction that "This will be a quality center with quality tenants. People in Bloomington are tired of going across town, fighting traffic, to College Mall. They want and deserve quality shopping and services on the west side. It's a logical site for a center . . . and it's ready to be built"? Perhaps you agree with Bill Finch, the attorney for the project. "It really is a good project. It opens up more of the west side in a meaningful way to more housing. The area needs upscale shopping, which is [sic] doesn't have right now. The infrastructure is there . . . it's a natural. The neighborhood and the business community are behind us on this and it compliments [sic] the push for more growth on the west side where there's room."[54]

What would you have done?

CHAPTER 18

Public Works

When it comes to city planning in a time of growth and sparse resources, what causes much friction between citizens and developers is a difference in priorities. For citizens, traffic matters most. For developers, water and sewage come first. And the question that builds the friction is, "Who will pay for the roads to carry our traffic to and fro; who will pay for the infrastructure to carry our water in, our sewage out?" How did our fast-growing town, under a ten-year state tax freeze, handle these extremely costly demands?

A major part of the burden fell on our Director of Public Works, Pat Patterson. Part of his job was to maintain the roads we already had, while improving arteries and intersections to the point where they could handle the additional traffic of our growing community. How did he get the necessary money?

First, he stretched the money already budgeted for roads by using in-house labor, equipment, and materials when possible. But his daring innovation was to use bond money for road improvements. In other words, we borrowed some of the necessary money. Citizens were willing to go along with the additional debt because roads were their top priority. The bond, a whopping $3.7 million, freed up some local money as a local match for additional federal dollars (on average, three dollars for every dollar of local money). In addition, he secured a federal grant to replace all city street signs.

In his spare time, Pat had to deal with another small problem, a legacy of one or more previous administrations. At some time before the McCloskey administration, the city began to provide water and sewer services to certain west side industries, outside the city limits, without requiring them to annex themselves to the city. As a result, they received city services but paid no city taxes.

My administration declared our intention to annex those west side industries. In response, they declared their intention to fight annexation in court. Instead, we worked out an agreement whereby they would pay the city, in lieu of annexation, a certain amount each year. In the meantime, the city would begin to annex property lying between the city limits and the industries. Our purpose there was to satisfy a state annexation requirement of contiguity between the city limits and the industries. This project would not be cheap, partly because of a state law that required us to upgrade any existing services to the same level as the prevailing city standard—and many of them were substandard (often lacking sewers).

Pat was always on the lookout for additional efficiencies. As it was very costly to deal with street flooding and backups, he strove to prevent them by repairing storm drains and inlets. City Utilities bought a sewer vacuum to remove sand and leaves, the major causes of clogging. In addition, he pushed a program to encourage residents to bag their leaves rather than raking them into the street to be washed down the drains. He started an in-house maintenance program to cut the downtime of city vehicles and equipment.

Patterson also supervised the Director of Sanitation, Ken Friedlander, whose dogged determination made a big success of our curbside recycling program (yard waste for composting, paper, glass, metals, and plastics). As I chaired the Environmental

Affairs Commission of Indiana Cities and Towns, I was proud indeed that Bloomington had both the first Tox-Away Day and the first curbside recycling program in the state. The city's Environmental Commission suggested these programs, and helped them to gain public acceptance.

Other infrastructure improvements came under the leadership of Mike Phillips, Director of Utilities, who budgeted $100,000 per year to replace old sewer and water lines in the older parts of town. His guiding philosophy: "Get them before they break!" Breakage was not the only problem he faced. Some water lines were too small to provide enough pressure for fire fighting. His program enabled us to tackle the large flooding problems presented by streams that flowed underground through the center of the city, Jordan River and Spanker's Branch.

To accommodate the rapid growth of our area and the increased demand for water, Utilities upgraded lift stations and boost stations and expanded the Monroe Water Treatment Plant. My predecessor, McCloskey, had secured a grant for the construction of a new sewage plant, and a new sewer line was planned for the Southwest Quadrant. The neighboring town of Ellettsville reaped major benefits from our improvements. When our Utilities department upgraded the Blucher Poole Wastewater Treatment Plant, the upgrade allowed Ellettsville to hook on, and thereby lift a sewer ban that had stopped all growth in that area.

We knew very well how sewer hook-ons could determine the direction of growth. Accordingly, our Utilities department, in the matter of hook-ons, honored our growth policy plan of compact urban form. We understood how important it was that Utilities and Planning work in harmony, and not at cross purposes.

City Utilities took the lead in our adoption of the Geographic Information System (GIS), and the assurance of compatibility with the county system. The GIS technology combines the graphic features of a map with information about other important specifications of the mapped area. It has proved to be an important resource for those concerned with area planning, problem solving, and decision making.

Public transit was another form of infrastructure that needed urgent, expert attention. When I became mayor in 1983 Bloomington's bus service had seen better days. After many ups and downs, it was limping along as best it could, which was none too good. Things were to change dramatically after 1985, when the Transit Board hired a highly capable professional, Dave Gionet, to direct Bloomington Transit. City transit systems get their money from federal grants, city taxes, and fares. When Gionet expanded the areas and hours of service, ridership rose dramatically, along with fare income. He initiated access service to the handicapped, and introduced kneeling buses.

He envisioned great efficiencies that could result if we would combine city and university bus systems, but found little enthusiasm among university officials. Nevertheless, he realized some efficiencies by scheduling city buses so as to complement the university schedules. And eventually the university, looking for efficiencies that would enable it to afford new equipment, finally agreed to share the city bus barn, a small step in the right direction.

CHAPTER 19

Facilitative Leadership

Soon after I left office we drove to Bronxville to visit old friends from graduate student days in Ann Arbor. Jim Doyle was intimately involved with New York City theater. His wife Charlotte, a psychology professor at Sarah Lawrence College, asked what it was like to lead a city. At the kitchen sink after dinner, as one washed and the other dried, we started a chat that would eventually set her on a mission to Bloomington for eyewitness accounts of my leadership in action. The fruit of her research was an unpublished manuscript she kindly shared with me. With her permission, I have made liberal use of her observations and insights in this chapter.

As I told her right away, and she repeated in her manuscript, "I didn't know that what I did had a name until I went to a conference on facilitative leadership." Charlotte checked its origin, and found that the term came from political science.[1]

In a nutshell, I led by striving to get my department heads whatever they needed to do their jobs well. I did not know all of the answers, and told them so; I would have to rely greatly on their initiative and creativity. I depended on the citizens and supported existing neighborhood associations. I encouraged the formation of new neighborhood associations, even helping them with the copying and mailing of their announcements. I appointed so many task forces that their profusion became a subject of amused comment. But they always came through; never was I disappointed with the product of a citizen task force.

I worked with the Bloomington Chamber of Commerce, which honored me with a Lifetime Achievement Award. I worked with local CEOs, and fostered many public-private partnerships to solve city problems. My way with a problem was to find people on all sides of an issue, get them around a table, and have them formulate a solution together. If someone complained about being left out, I would put that person at the table. Nobody knew everything, but many knew something. The trick was to find out who they were and get them working together in a productive direction.

This facilitative style of leadership came partly from my experience as a community volunteer, which began when my younger daughter started school. I tutored children and worked in community development. During the Vietnam War I joined a women's peace group. The problem with every group was to keep it focused on a particular action, and I fell into the role of consensus finder.

Consensus alone was not enough. Once you had one you had to carry it out, and the ones to do that work were volunteers. I know of exceptions, but in the typical volunteer group you cannot get very far by coming in and issuing marching orders. The great thing was that everybody was willing to do something. They would say "I have writing talents," or "I'll just work the telephone," or "I'll bring the food," or "I'll baby sit." And I was the organizer. I would not go out and get the baby sitters, but select the baby sitter chairperson, who would. Someone had to think about the proposed action as a whole, and that's what I would do.

People are often reluctant to tackle a big problem, so I would divide it up into manageable pieces. I'd say, "Three of you together can do this, and let's see what else needs to be done." Somebody had to figure out how to divide the task and get the parts done, because otherwise it would look impossibly complicated. As I did not have all of the necessary skills, I relied on others to do the various parts, and they would step forward. Often bargaining was necessary, so I'd figure out what they were willing to do, then try to get them whatever help they needed.

Different groups had different ways of deciding what to do. The League of Women Voters would always do extensive research before taking a position on an issue. Women's International League for Peace and Freedom had a national organization that would suggest particular directions, but members of each local branch would decide what their branch would do.

I did volunteer work for many different groups, from Community Development Conference to Citizens for Good Government, and learned something of value from each one. But it was my work with various peace groups that took me into elective politics and the nitty gritty of organizing political campaigns. I learned a lot when our friend Jim Dinsmoor ran for Congress on a peace platform in the Democratic primary of 1966; we lost in the district, but won in Monroe County. Two years later, when Senator Eugene McCarthy ran in the primaries against President Johnson, I played a big role in McCarthy's Monroe County campaign. But all of my volunteer experience was an essential part of my later political career.

Even before he became I.U. student body vice president, Jeff Richardson and I worked together on several causes. Years later he was elected to the Bloomington City Council. When a fellow councilman resigned, Jeff persuaded the others, some quite dubious, that I was the best person to fill the vacancy.

On the council I continued what I had learned as a volunteer. If an issue needed research, I would do it or have it done. I listened. A small group of constituents, led by Tom and Polly Dixon, were concerned about the appearance and cleanliness of their neighborhood and the city. When we thought we needed an ordinance to improve matters I appealed for help from Clean

Cities, a national organization that knew quite a lot about the issue. I approached the mayor's department heads, and asked how the council could help them do their jobs more effectively. And I found myself again in the familiar role of consensus maker.

To quote Charlotte Doyle: "By now, her leadership in the council was recognized both by the voters and by her peers. Tomi was elected council-member-at-large in the next local election. And the members of city council voted her city council president. When the mayor of the city was elected to Congress, Tomi was selected by the precinct committee to complete the mayor's term. Subsequently the voters elected her mayor in the next three elections."

As I told Charlotte, on my first day as mayor I walked into City Hall and asked myself, "How the heck do you run this place?" But the only way that felt comfortable was the way I learned as a volunteer leader. This particular group was composed of city department heads—the comptroller, the public works director, the corporation counsel and others—many of whom I knew from city council days. I made new hires. I encouraged them to take their own initiatives, which I would find ways to support.

Charlotte quoted me: "I hired people who had ideas of their own and they often would coincide with the directions we were heading in. I would let them develop their ideas and run with them. So they were in effect working on their own projects, rather than on my projects. Glenda Murray came in with a long interest in redevelopment . . . something she really cared about . . . it was thrilling for her to have a chance to do it." As the corporation counsel told Charlotte, "You had ownership of what you did."

That was not quite true. As decisions often had consequences that crossed departmental lines, it was simply not realistic to let department heads operate independently, as they had been doing, and often in competition for city resources. I formed a cooperative team of my city officials, the "A-team," that met with me weekly to discuss issues that required coordinated action. Any necessary research was done before the meeting, anyone could disagree without fear of reprisal, and we often reached a consensus. Even when we did not, the team members felt that the issue and the possible courses of action had been aired thoroughly. I would then organize the group for action, and members would volunteer for various tasks and promise completion dates.

The A-team's courses of action did not just bubble up out of free wheeling brainstorm sessions. In my very first year in office, under my leadership the A-team agreed on a list of general priorities. The infrastructure had been neglected, and needed a lot of work. Roads were in bad shape, and we had to fix them. The same for parks and other recreational facilities. It was absolutely essential to restore the downtown. We desperately needed a new city hall, but that would have to wait. So we had a general program early on and a sense of what would have to come first, and we had to find a way to implement the program.

Typically I would come into an A-team meeting with a pretty clear notion of what I wanted done, and I would tell them about it. It would go on from there, with various team members putting their oars in as they saw fit. I would look for common threads, try to pull them together, and thereby shape both the group discussion and the eventual city policy.

Linda Runkel, Corporation Counsel, told Charlotte: "As we came to a conclusion on issues, she talked about what the next step would be. You knew what was expected of you when you left the room. Each of us knew our strengths and weaknesses. So when you assign what comes next, 'Linda you do this,' it didn't feel assigned. One comptroller was a visionary, invented creative financing. I would take his wild ideas and make them legal. He was not an attention to details guy. So details were assigned to someone else like me—a stickler for details."

I strove for group cohesion, between and within departments, in my hiring practice. I never hired anyone on my own. If a key vacancy came up in some department, I would figure out what other departments the replacement would have to work with, and all of the departments involved would take part in the selection of the replacement.

The group discussions made us more daring. Charlotte Doyle had heard this both from me and many A-teamers. "The comptroller spoke of the terrifying decisions that have to be made in city government and the security that came from a thorough discussion. Tomi, in comparing her administration to the previous one, which did not differ in political philosophy, spoke of being more aggressive in taking on expensive projects using a risky tactic, increasing taxes in an era of cuts in federal grants to cities and citizen tax revolts."

Charlotte thought that another characteristic of the citizen volunteer, devotion to cause rather than personal wealth, fame or ambition, was apparent in my leadership style. Reverend Ernie Butler said, "There was nothing personal she wanted to gain." But she also quoted my older daughter, Devon, who expressed some frustration with this virtue. Devon said, "She doesn't think about what's good for her or at least she thinks first about other things. She doesn't think first, will this help me get elected next year, is this going to make people think I am brilliant. Is this going to make people think I am a good mayor. It used to drive us crazy. I can't think of another politician whose staff they appoint wouldn't be out working for them to get reelected. In a way it's stupid. You need those people to really work. No, you need those people to be really good at what their job is. It was all about making a difference, making things better." Charlotte also quoted my saying, "I was always proud to be mayor of Bloomington . . . because we were doing it . . . . [Other cities] copied our programs. Our people were called on all the time to lead seminars. They knew they were good. Linda won an award. Utilities won an award, parks . . . human resources for social service programs . . . the police chief . . . ."

How did we know what would make things better? City employees knew quite a lot, from the ground up to the department heads, about what would need to be done. So did citizens. That would explain a practice invented in my first citywide mayoral campaign that some thought quirky or phony. As we went door to door we would hand voters a postcard addressed to me that they could fill out at their leisure to tell me their concerns.

To take just one example, that was how we knew that voters were so concerned about the condition of city streets, that road repair had to be a top priority. It also told us how we might finance the project. We had never floated bonds for road repairs, but the public works director suggested that we consider this new strategy. Now, bond issues are risky, and require a lot of work. Voters have to petition to put the issue on the ballot, and a majority must vote in favor of the issue. The reason it seemed risky was that the bonds would have to be paid off with tax money. But I already knew which roads were of concern in each neighborhood, and the bonding plan took these concerns into account. I believed that if the plan were created with care, and reflected voters' needs, the voters would support it. And indeed they did.

This desire to listen would also explain my open door policy. If the mayor was in, her door was open to anyone who wanted to drop in, city employees and citizens alike. Some simply wanted a chat. Others had a particular gripe or problem I might help them resolve. These casual drop-ins could make my office staff nervous. Sometimes they made me nervous; not all of my visitors were perfectly balanced. However, I never regretted the open door; I learned a lot from the conversations that ensued, and sometimes managed to improve an individual life. One memorable lady, who had had great difficulty keeping a roof over her head, dropped in and stated her problem. Decades later she still wrote me at Christmas, with thanks for having helped her secure a place of her own.

Where did my kind of facilitative leadership come from? It's easier to say where it did not come from. It did not come from a book. It did not come from a political science course at Occidental College. It did not come from a revered mentor. It came from a more diffuse source, from growing up in a small town in the San Joaquin Valley.

Madera was a community in every sense of the word. The people who lived there were closely interwoven with one another and the town's institutions, a town of their own making. The community was its people, as Jane Jacobs wrote many years later. I had seen that for myself as I grew up in Madera. I saw my surroundings—the schools, the houses, the downtown, the barren or tree-lined avenues—as a consensual history of the town.

But I had seen too that certain segments of the population claimed a bigger stake in the community than others. Was that fair? Didn't we all live in the same community? How could we claim to have a genuine community if any of its segments had little power to shape the town, to make it more livable on its own terms? When I grew up and moved around the country—Fresno, Los Angeles, Claremont, Upland, Ann Arbor—wherever I went I saw a consensual history of place, with some of its people left out of the consensus.

When I came to Bloomington it seemed that much of the west side had been left out. It seemed that city government, with its zoning policy, had ruined other vibrant parts of the community by permitting the construction of apartment houses in the midst of family neighborhoods. Had anyone bothered to ask what these residents wanted?

In Bloomington one of my first volunteer activities involved the tutoring of poor children. That led to my work in organizing Community Development Conference, an effort to empower west side residents. As a direct result Reverend Ernest Butler decided to run for township trustee, and other west siders soon followed his lead. Given this background, it should have been no surprise when the new Mayor Allison reached out to the black community. Butler told Charlotte Doyle that the blacks, who had formerly felt excluded from decision-making and denied their share of city resources, now felt included. "The west side didn't count. Tomi changed it. We became a part of the city."

Another example of leading by listening was a program called "Kid City." It started when I heard many city employees complain about the lack of the summer day care that was absolutely essential if they were to continue their jobs with the city. We thought of a day care facility funded and run by the city, but found the prospect too costly.

Chance intervened as we interviewed candidates to head the city parks department. One candidate happened to mention that his own city's parks department ran a summer day care program. The flash bulb went off. We had a fine parks department, with good resources and good staff, but institutional opposition to any such notion. The parks department was not supposed to do any baby-sitting. No way.

I did not order anyone to shape up or ship out. I did have a talk with our new parks director, Norm Merrifield. I pointed out that he was blessed with excellent staff, resources and financial support. I told him I really wanted a summer day care program, for the sake of both city employees and the many other citizens with the same pressing need. I asked him to talk it over with his staff and see what kind of solution they could come up with.

Lo and behold, one of his staffers came up with Kid City, a truly innovative prize-winner, that fit the parks philosophy. This was and remains a summer day care program administered by the city parks department, designed to familiarize the children with city resources. For example, it gave them firsthand experience with use of the city bus system, and use of the county library. We hoped it would help working parents, and help their children become part of the city.

The same spirit motivated our affordable housing program for working families, and our Self Sufficiency program. The latter program, rather than simply mandate work, helped clients get to work by helping them solve their housing, child care and transportation problems.

My administration was not an unbroken line of successes. Where did it work, where did it fail, and why?

One of our biggest success stories was the arrest of downtown decay. As had happened in other cities, when malls appeared on the outskirts stores deserted the center, leaving their beautiful old buildings to the slow rot of vacancy. When I became mayor several groups were doing their separate best, mostly in vain, to stop the deterioration of the downtown. There was a group devoted to preservation of historic buildings. There were businessmen, born and bred in Bloomington, saddened to witness the decline of their city's center. There were neighborhood activists who lived near the downtown. Mayor McCloskey had built a parking garage for Bill Cook's Graham Hotel remodeling, but no other private investors followed suit. It was one of those big, complex problems, maybe too hard to solve.

First I hired a director expert in downtown redevelopment and passionately devoted to the cause. We found a national organization, Main Street, that was also devoted to downtown restoration. I appointed a citizen task force—all stake holders, but with many different interests—and put them with the redevelopment director for discussion, research and planning. The director pulled their ideas together and emerged with a consensus on a Main Street plan to facilitate central redevelopment.

The plan specified the creation of a commission to encourage private and public activities downtown. It encouraged the development of downtown housing to attract residents to the center. The city would take part through its role in zoning and tax abatement policies. Because parking was a major problem, the city would also spend some of its precious resources to build parking structures. We would invest more in downtown streets and parks. Our tax abatement policies would encourage investment in the center. We would cooperate with the county in renovating the focal point of the old downtown, the county courthouse. We would sponsor events to bring more people downtown.

Little by little, more business people joined the cause. Today it is widely agreed that downtown redevelopment was a major achievement of city government.

Planning and zoning was another problem that seemed impossibly difficult at first. This one involved a fierce conflict between neighborhood activists and the business community, partly about the location of neighborhood shopping centers in residential areas. As the problem stemmed largely from zoning regulations of the 1960s, the solution required a new master plan for zoning—a formidable task that our planning department viewed with great trepidation.

The key was to invite all segments of the community, including residents of low-income neighborhoods, to put in their two cents' worth. As I told Charlotte Doyle, "I struggled long and hard to bring in people who usually didn't have a chance. It's not easy because they are not used to it . . . they are working long hard hours. Transportation is always a problem. We worked to make it easy by making meetings close to where they lived, making it more convenient."

At a memorable meeting designed for a different constituency, staged in a local high school, irate developers accused me of holding foregone conclusions that would devalue property, already purchased in good faith, by now forbidding its commercial development. I told them I was there to listen, and would listen to everyone. This particular consensus would have to involve the whole city.

At long last we did arrive at a consensus, a plan crafted by a smaller group of people who represented all of the various constituencies. All property registered by a certain date could keep its present zoning. However, in the future all property sold in now-residential neighborhoods would be rezoned against further commercial development. It was a compromise in which no constituency got everything, but every constituency got something it wanted.

In spite of all the consultation, some members of the community remained unhappy with the solution, and broadcast their displeasure far and wide. Businessmen who resented any limitation on commercial development formed a group to dismantle the new master plan. When she drove into Bloomington, Charlotte Doyle saw a relic of their intention, a billboard that warned: "PROTECT YOUR PROPERTY RIGHTS AGAINST MAYOR ALLISON . . . ."

In the heat of that past moment the newspaper too expressed a fear that the new plan might curtail city development. But by the time I left office it had changed its tune. "The slow thorough process by which the plan and ordinance were adopted truly was community inclusive, and though some still grumble about both, they are working pretty much as they were designed to work."[2]

The iconic building of my administration is the new city hall in the Showers complex. After several meetings with the A-team, I decided that the enormous old Showers furniture factory was the best solution to our city hall problem, the cramped quarters and the city departments scattered all over town. I knew it would take a monumental effort to get the three necessary constituencies together—the city for its city hall, Indiana University for a research park, and a private developer for shops and offices.

Showers had many pros and cons. It sat in an underdeveloped area on the boundary between downtown and the west side, and could help tie them together. It offered a huge amount of space, but was run down. Indiana University, the owner, used it only for storage, and had done little upkeep. Its wonderful zigzag roof line admitted gobs of natural light. It shared a neighborhood with I.U. Press, itself in a former Showers building, and begged for historic preservation.

It had severe critics. Charlotte Doyle cited the thoughts of a Republican council member. "Why would anybody want to be in that hole. The street was as low as you could get in Bloomington. The building was falling apart." My first big job was to bring the city council around. Charlotte quoted my daughter, Devon. "It was a devil to organize to get that thing to happen. She worked on that for years. No one else could have done it . . . no one." The president of the corporation that developed the private section said, "It was like herding kittens. She got all the people headed in the right direction." The corporation counsel, who did much of the city's work on the project, added, "She knew it could be done, that it would take a lot of patience, perseverance, persistence, and hard work, and it did. This was one of the many, many great accomplishments of her administration." The skeptical council member, who came to head the nonprofit financing effort, said, "I wrote six million dollars worth of checks. It's a gem." Further, "I was park board president for sixteen years. We built a magnificent park program. I think we were all proud we were in government [during] the time the city progressed. Bloomington bustled."

The Showers complex connected downtown and the west side, won lavish architectural recognition, became home to a thriving Saturday farmers' market, and stands as a major city landmark.

The new city hall was completed in November, 1995, about six weeks before my final term ended. From the vantage point of my office in the new city hall, I relished those weeks like few others.

My greatest frustration was our community's failure to solve our PCB problem. Because PCBs have long since fallen out of our daily news, many may think the problem has been solved. It has not. The "solution" finally adopted was to cap the PCBs in place, treat the water runoff, and hope for the best. As long as the PCBs remain in place, so does the problem, with its continuing threat of systemic contamination.

The corporation that put them there in the first place would have been delighted with that solution all along. I never thought it worthy of celebration.

To understand its origin, one must start with the fact that authority over Superfund cleanups abided with the EPA. Under prevailing Superfund law local government could not override EPA cleanup decisions. The McCloskey administration sued in an effort to acquire some say in the cleanup, and won a Consent Decree that empowered our Utilities Service Board to veto any cleanup method proven to be a threat to public health. It was the first time a locality had gained such a power, and none has gained it since.

In the Consent Decree Westinghouse proposed incineration, but held open the option of other methods that might come along in the future. Opponents of incineration first tried to kill the Consent Decree, but later began to tout other methods, none of which panned out. I defended the Consent Decree because it indemnified the taxpayer, held Westinghouse liable, and provided the only way that locals could have some say over the cleanup.

As things turned out, our Utilities Service Board never had to determine the safety of incineration. Before it came to that, the EPA accepted the present method: Cap in place, treat the runoff, and hope for the best. This represented a huge departure from the EPA's initial requirement of a total cleanup. Thus, our limited local authority meant that an action could be stopped, but no real cleanup achieved.

My political opponents took full advantage of the opportunity. They found it easy to demonize incineration and, by association, both the Consent Decree and its defenders. They called me an advocate of incineration. They ignored my reply that I advocated local control, not incineration. They picketed city hall, shouted me down, attacked me in the newspaper as an enemy of the environment, and put up posters that compared me with

Hitler. Later, when I opposed a new GE incinerator because it failed to meet EPA standards, my political problem vanished, but the PCBs stayed in the ground. They are still there.

Inside my administration it was not all sweetness and light, as Charlotte Doyle attested. "The city council sometimes chafed at a moralistic stance. 'She was tough on what she wanted to get done. I've seen her with the burr up ready to fight for what she wanted. She put her fist down and somehow it got done.' In the day-to-day work, one member of her staff told me of a time when 'we were screaming at one another,' and another spoke of 'times we could have clobbered her,' and also of times when 'she could have clobbered us.' But the dominant tone of every interview was respect and affection for Tomi, recognition of her sensitivity and patience, and deep pride in what was accomplished."

The comptroller chimed in, "I worked for a woman who fostered an environment of be all that you can be . . . I didn't just want to do the money. I wanted to be part of actually making that project happen, getting the fire station built, picking the architect. The capital projects committee did lots of stuff with lots of impact and I got to chair it. No matter how long I am gone, I will always drive into that square and go 'look at what we did.' It is probably just a small percentage of the population [who] can go through a community and know they were part of what stands before them, a good thing for the people who live there."

I told Charlotte about my inner compass. "I call it a plumb line. Builders always use a plumb line to keep a balance so you make sure that you are not tilting off, that you are upright. There is certain right and there is certain wrong. And that is how you behave whether it is to your advantage or to your disadvantage. Always keep your word. And always treat people with respect, even your enemy. You do not cheat; you do not lie . . . you do not embarrass people."

I will always cherish my years as Bloomington's mayor. I think of the carolers who dropped by our house every Christmas season. Right now I cherish my years as Bloomington's former mayor and the many friends and strangers who stop me on the street or in the grocery store and thank me for what I did for the city.

Reverend Ernie Butler will have the last word, from his interview with Charlotte Doyle: "We worked together cooperatively helping to upgrade disadvantaged persons who haven't had the opportunity for fulfilling their potential. We were a melting pot."

Former Mayor Allison opens the Allison Juke-box Community Center June, 2000 (Allison, Fernandez, Renneisen) (uncredited photo)

Tomi leaves office, 1995 (photo by James Allison).

Notes

CHAPTER 4
THE CAMPAIGN TRAIL, MILE 4

1. Mary Dieter, *Louisville Courier-Journal*, January 6, 1983. "Bloomington has new mayor—finally."
2. Brian Werth, *Bloomington Herald-Telephone*, December 30, 1982. "Memories and visions. McCloskey reminisces on mayoral years, looks forward to role in Washington."
3. H-T Staff Report, Ibid., December 27, 1982. "Eyes on McCloskey."
4. Kyle Richmond, *Indiana Daily Student*, January 6, 1983. "A new mayor."

CHAPTER 6
DENVER SMITH

1. Personal communication, former officer Steve Sharp, December 10, 2009.
2. State Star Report, *Indianapolis Star*, September 28, 1983.
3. Laura Lane, *Bloomington Herald-Times*, September 7, 2003.
4. Ibid., September 3, 2003.
5. *Indianapolis Star*, September 28,1983. "Policeman tells hearing he should have fired more shots."
6. Ed Bond, *Indiana Daily Student*, February 12, 1988. "Officer recalls final shots fired at Smith."

7. Laura Lane, *Bloomington Herald-Telephone*, February 17, 1988. "Smith suit, a final chapter: police hope life will resume."
8. Mary O'Doherty, *Louisville Courier-Journal*, September 16, 1983.
9. Dan Kadlec, *Bloomington Herald-Telephone*, September 18, 1983.
10. *Indiana Daily Student*, September 22, 1983.
11. Ann Wesley, Ibid., October 5, 1983.
12. Francine Grant and Mark Rochester, Ibid., September 26, 1983, "Marchers question shooting."
13. Dan Kadlec, *Bloomington Herald-Telephone*, September 27 and September 29, 1983, "Public comment critical of police in Smith shooting."
14. Ibid., Dec. 4, 1980.
15. *Indianapolis News*, September 24, 1983.
16. Laura Lane, *HeraldTimesOnline*.com, September 7, 2003, "The death of Denver Smith."
17. Tim Baker, *Indiana Daily Student*, November 7, 1983. "Protesters march on city hall to remember Smith's death."
18. Mary O'Doherty, *Louisville Courier-Journal*, 1983. "Ohio group will probe Denver Smith shooting."
19. Madeline Strong, *Indiana Daily Student*, January 16, 1984. "Protesters removed from service after interrupting Allison's speech."
20. Bill Strother, *Bloomington Herald-Telephone*, June 15, 1984. "Denver Smith's widow files $5 million lawsuit."
21. *Star State Report, Indianapolis Star*, February 16, 1984. "U.S. ends probe of athlete's death."
22. Laura Lane, *Bloomington Herald-Telephone*, February 16, 1988. "Police cleared in Smith case. Police shooting 'was wrong,' widow says after jury's verdict."
23. *Herald-Telephone Report*, May 6, 1988. "Cynequa Smith drops verdict appeal."

24. Laura Lane, *Bloomington Herald-Times*, September 7, 2003. "Promise kept: Smith's daughter a junior at IU.

CHAPTER 7
THE CAMPAIGN TRAIL, MILE 6

1. Brian Werth, *Bloomington Herald-Telephone*, January 10, 1983. "Mayor Tomi Allison starts to define her administration."
2. Ibid., October 18, 1983. "No surprises in mayoral forum."
3. Ibid., November 4, 1983. "Mayor: Tomi Allison."

CHAPTER 9
THE CAMPAIGN TRAIL, MILES 7 AND 8

1. Steve Hinnefield, *Bloomington Herald-Telephone*, May 6, 1987. "Allison survives Zietlow's assault."
2. Ibid., May 6, 1987. "Divisions in party a new challenge for Democrats."
3. Ibid., March 3, 1984.
4. Jackie Sheckler, *Bloomington Herald-Times*, January 16, 1992. "Vazsonyi's campaign outspent Allison 2-1." The information about the financing of the 1987 election did not appear in the newspaper until this article by Sheckler in 1992.
5. Steve Hinnefield, *Bloomington Herald-Telephone*, June 18, 1987. "Ellis wants to hire scientist to oversee city's PCB cleanup."
6. Ibid., August 3, 1987. "Towell says consent decree changes needed."
7. Julie Creek, Ibid., July 20, 1987. "Andrews seeks referendum to abolish city utilities board."
8. Liz Brown, *Indiana Daily Student*, September 11, 1987. "Problems don't quench Allison's desire for job."

9. Steve Hinnefield, *Bloomington Herald-Telephone*, October 23, 1987. "Debates bring hot crossfire in mayor race."

10. Ibid., November 4, 1987. "Allison edges out Ellis. Mayor reelected in four-way race."

11. Our opinion, Ibid., November 5, 1987. "Allison won and lost Tuesday."

12. Your opinion, Ibid., November 11, 1987. "H-T editorials too harsh on mayor."

CHAPTER 10
PLEASANTRIES

1. Linda Thomas, *Bloomington Herald-Telephone*, May 19, 1989. "Bench marks—Mayor invites area stone carvers to enter contest."

2. Ibid., September 9, 1989. "Dinosaur wins, invites adventure."

CHAPTER 11
THE CAMPAIGN TRAIL, MILES 9 AND 10

1. Jackie Sheckler, *Bloomington Herald-Telephone*, May 1, 1991. "Mayoral candidates enter home stretch of primary campaign."

2. Ibid., May 8, 1991. "Fielder to face Allison. Mayor soundly defeats opponents in primary."

3. Laura Lane and Jackie Sheckler, Ibid., June 27, 1991. "Fielder quits Bloomington mayor's race."

4. John Langley, Your Opinion, Ibid., October 16, 1991. "TV ad corrected."

5. Jackie Sheckler, Ibid., January 16, 1992. "Vazsonyi's campaign outspent Allison 2-1."

6. Ibid., November 6, 1991. "Tomi Allison wins reelection in rout. Mayor gets 50.5% in three-way race."

CHAPTER 12
DOWNTOWN

1. Jane Jacobs.*The Death and Life of American Cities.* New York: Random House, 1961.

CHAPTER 13
ARTS AND CRAFT

1. Will Counts and John Dilts. *The Magnificent 92: Indiana Courthouses.* Bloomington, IN: Rosebud Press, 1991. Reprinted by Indiana University Press in 1999.
2. Carolyn Kramer, *Indiana Daily Student* , May 1, 1981.
3. Kurt Van der Dussen, *Bloomington Herald-Telephone,* November 7, 1982.
4. Paul Carmony, Letter to the Editor, Ibid., November 7, 1982.
5. Authors' interview of Rosemary Miller, July 2, 2009.

CHAPTER 15
SOCIAL NEEDS

1. Brent Christensen, *Bloomington Herald-Times,* September 14, 1992.

CHAPTER 16
THE SHOWERS PROJECT

1. Much of this information comes from *A History of the Showers Furniture Company of Bloomington, Indiana, 1869-1955.* Unpublished manuscript by Dan Hirsch, April 14, 1977. Irene Neu. On deposit in the Indiana Room, Monroe County Library, Bloomington, Indiana.
2. Brian Werth, *Bloomington Herald-Times,* July 9, 1989.
3. Kurt Van der Dussen, Ibid., August 27, 1989.
4. Julie Creek, Ibid., January 19, 1990.

5. Ibid., April 2, 1990.
6. Ibid., April 14, 1990.
7. Ibid., April 19, 1990.
8. Teri Klassen, Ibid., June 10, 1990.
9. Stephen Beaven, Ibid., April 26, 1990.
10. Jackie Sheckler, Ibid., December 14, 1990.
11. Ibid., December 22, 1990.
12. Nick Sutcliffe, *Indiana Daily Student*, February 21, 1991.
13. Jackie Sheckler, *Bloomington Herald-Times*, May 16, 1992.
14. Ibid., May 30, 1992.
15. J.R. Ross, *Indiana Daily Student*, October 7, 1993.
16. David Thompson, *Bloomington Herald-Times*, December 11, 1993.
17. Jackie Sheckler, Ibid., September 19, 1993.
18. Steve Hinnefield, Ibid., November 3, 1995.
19. *Architectural Record*, February, 1996.
20. Jackie Sheckler, *Bloomington Herald-Times*, November 15, 1995.
21. Ibid., April 7, 1994.
22. Meghan Hoyer, *Bloomington Herald-Times*, July 13, 1996.

CHAPTER 17
PLANNING AND ZONING

1. Julie Creek, *Bloomington Herald-Times*, May 18, 1990. "City issues highlighted in survey." Our Opinion, *Bloomington Herald-Times*, May 18, 1990.
2. Ibid., May 20, 1990. "Master land plan gets airing out."
3. Ibid., July 15, 1990. "Growth study gets mixed reviews."
4. Ibid., July 30, 1990. "Bloomington planners want public input for master plan."
5. Ibid., October 9, 1990. "Growth topic for planning meeting."

6. Ibid., February 27, 1991. "New city master plan to be unveiled."
7. Ibid., March 22, 1991. "Many offer master plan feedback."
8. Tim Jackson, *Bloomington Herald-Times*, March 5, 1991. "Citizens critique [sic] city plan."
9. Jackie Sheckler, *Bloomington Herald-Times*, March 25, 1991. "Master plan protecting family areas."
10. Ibid., March 21, 1991. "Master plan debate focuses on restricting east-side growth."
11. Our opinion editorial, *Bloomington Herald-Times*, March 28, 1991. "Master plan good, not perfect."
12. Jackie Sheckler, *Bloomington Herald-Times*, April 16, 1991. "City plan commission approves master plan."
13. Ibid., May 16, 1991. "Council approves master plan."
14. Ibid., August 27, 1991. Untitled.
15. Ibid., September 19, 1991. "Neighbors fight development plan."
16. Ibid., September 20, 1991. "Council OKs shopping center—master plan gets credit, blame for project approval."
17. Ibid., September 22, 1991. "Manager to enforce master plan's guidelines."
18. Ibid., September 24, 1991. "Mayor vetoes new shopping complex—Surprise move stuns council members."
19. Ibid., October 3, 1991. "Kinser Pike shopping center gets go-ahead despite mayor's move."
20. Ibid., October 25, 1991. "Master plan big issue in election."
21. Ibid., October 30, 1991. "Master plan key issue for at-large candidates."
22. Ibid., November 19, 1991. "Master plan key issue for at-large candidates."
23. Ibid., December 12, 1991. "First vote goes against shopping center proposal."

24. Steve Hinnefield, *Bloomington Herald-Times*, December 19, 1991. "Rogers Farm plan rejected—Council votes 8-1 against Rechter development request."
25. Our opinion editorial, Ibid., January 2, 1992.
26. Robert Niles, *Bloomington Herald-Times*, January 9, 1992. "Henke proposal divides council."
27. Jackie Sheckler, Ibid., January 16, 1992. "Henke housing project OK'd."
28. Ibid., January 13, 1992. "Planners to discuss condos."
29. Robert Niles, *Bloomington Herald-Times*, January 14, 1992. "Planners hear pros, cons of development on Hillside."
30. Jackie Sheckler, Ibid., February 8, 1992. "Growth by design—Bloomington part of mayors' institute."
31. Jennifer Thelen, Ibid., February 20, 1992. "Southside dwellers do some planning."
32. Jackie Sheckler, Ibid., April 22, 1992. "Rezoning plan sent back for revision."
33. Steve Hinnefield, Ibid., May 2, 1992. "Wal-Mart, Sam's Club look at west side site."
34. Jackie Sheckler, *Bloomington Herald-Times*, May 21, 1992. "Parking to change Aug. 15."
35. Ibid., June 23, 1992. "Mayor forms citizens' panel to advise on master plan."
36. Ibid., July 31, 1993. "New draft for rezoning ready."
37. Andy Dworkin, *Bloomington Herald-Times*, August 6, 1993. "Plan commission gets look at new city zoning ordinance."
38. Matthew Watson, *Bloomington Herald-Times*, February 8, 1994. "Master plan audit draws complaints."
39. Ibid., February 23, 1994. "High-rise well-received by planners, public."
40. Ibid., March 22, 1994. "Planners give conditional OK to planned CFC high-rise."

41. Jackie Sheckler, *Bloomington Herald-Times*, April 22, 1994. "Cook plans to drop project."

42. Ibid., March 24, 1994. "Deadline for zoning rules set."

43. Ibid., June 2, 1994. "Article attacks city's Growth Policies Plan."

44. Rex Buntain, *Bloomington Herald-Times*, November 8, 1994. "Committee: Growth plan will cause housing shortage."

45. Marian Young, Ibid., November 21, 1994. "Mayor will announce political plants [sic] today. Democratic and Republican hopefuls look to May primary."

46. *Bloomington Herald-Times*, November 26, 1994. "Our opinion editorial—City ready for change at the top."

47. Jackie Sheckler, Ibid., December 27, 1994. "Zoning proposal ready for viewing."

48. *Bloomington Herald-Times*, January 20, 1995. "Mayor's speech sets good tone."

49. Jackie Sheckler, Ibid., April 5, 1995. "Final council vote tonight on city zoning ordinance. Public comment to precede vote on document four years in the making."

50. Our opinion editorial, Ibid., April 19, 1995. "Ordinance in place, now make it work."

51. Jackie Sheckler, *Bloomington Herald-Times*, June 21, 1995. "Few object to new development."

52. Ibid., June 22, 1995. "New shopping center up for vote."

53. "Council votes 6-1 to approve new shopping center." Our opinion editorial, *Bloomington Herald-Times*, June 23, 1995. "Whitehall Crossing vote was on the mark."

54. Brian Werth, Ibid., May 21,1995. "Whitehall Crossing is on track. Strip Mall for west side may bring upscale megastores, cinema."

CHAPTER 19
FACILITATIVE LEADERSHIP

1. J. H. Svara and Associates. *Facilitative Leadership in Local Government*. San Francisco: Jossey-Bass, 1994.
2. Mayor Allison leaves community stronger." *Bloomington Herald-Times*, December 30, 1995.

Index

(Italicized page numbers indicate photos)

A

Adult education, 141
Affordable housing, 88, 136, 137-139, 161, 177, 181-182, 202
Allison
    Devon, 5, 6, 15, 33, 48, *50*, 199, 206
    James (Jim), 5, 6, 15, 18, *50*, 68-71, 74, 79, 80-81, *84*, 85, 86,
        152, 209
    Leigh, 5, 6, 15, 18, *50*
    Tomi, 2-5, *11*, 12, 16, 33, *34*, *44*, *46*, 47, 48, *50, 52*, 64, 68, 69,
        70, 74, 81, *84*, 89, 90, *93*, 118, 121, 148, *150, 151, 152*, 176,
        197, 199, 202, 208, *209*
    Tomilea, 2, 12, *50*
Allen, Ross, 26
Alternative Transportation Fund, 175
American Federation of State, County, and Municipal Employ-
    ees (AFSCME), 91
Amethyst, 140
Anderson
    Norm, 118
    Road Landfill, 57
Andrews
    Mike, 71, 72
    Moya, 46

Ann Arbor. *See* Michigan
Annexation, 191
Annual Limestone Symposium, 127
Antigrowth, 172, 181
Architectural Record, 151
Atkins, Mike, 29

B

B-Line Trail, 104, 136
Bailey, Mike, 165
Baker
    Mary, 117
    Mike, 89
Ball State University, 31
Ballew, C. H., 145
Ballinger
    Art Center, 85
    Edna, 126
Banneker Community Center, 131
Barker, Bob, 148
Barnes, Ruth C., 114
Batman, 67
Baude, Patrick, 32, 37
Baumgartner, Madeline, 153, *154*
Baxter, Penny, 85
Beard, Ben, 162
Beautification, 99, 183
Bedford, 68, 69, 70, 71, 83, 85
Bennett Stone Quarry, 54
Black Elks Lodge, 45
Black roses, 172

Bloomington

Advancement Corporation (BAC), 148, 149, 151

Area Arts Council, 105, 108

Board of Public Safety, 32, 33, 35, 38, 40, 41

Board of Public Works, 149

Chamber of Commerce, 49, 143, 164, 181, 184, 195

City Council, 7, 11, 12, 13, 18, 19, 44, 47, 54, 55, 67, 68, 72, 73, 90, 91, 92, 94, 99, 123, 126, 127, 130, 144, 147, 148, 149, 150, 153, 155, 159, 160, 163, 164, 165, 169, 170, 173, 175, 178, 179, 184, 185, 186, 187, 188, 196, 197, 206, 208

City Hall, 16, 17, 19, 20, 21, 25, 26, 27, 39, 48, 50, 55, 68, 73, 78, 88, 92, 96, 101, 103, 104, 105, 107, 108, 120, 131, 135, 137, 142, 143, 147-152, 197, 198, 205, 206, 207, 209. *See also* Municipal Building

Dental Clinic, 140

Elections

1977, 11

1979, 12

1983, 15-18

1987, 58, 60

1991, 60, 88

Municipal Facilities Corporation, 149

Origin of name, 6

Plan

Commission, 156, 157, 163, 164, 169, 186, 187, 188

Director, 158

Police Advisory Board, 32

Public

Transit, 49, 158, 163, 176, 193

Works, 100, 105, 124, 129, 136, 149, 190-193

Redevelopment, 49, 71, 99-106, 136-138, 161, 166, 197, 203-204

Restorations, Inc. (BRI), 115, 121

Traffic Commission, 179

Bloomington
  Herald-Telephone, 48, 50, 62, 70, 71, 73, 74, 90, 91, 100, 112-120
  Herald-Times, 112, 162, 172, 180, *182*, 183, 184, 187
Bloomington High School North, 32
Bloomington High School South (BHS), 158
Blucher Poole Wastewater Treatment Plant, 192
Bonds, 112, 114, 115, 116, 117, 119, 120, 123, 128, 130, 131, 148, 149, 190, 200
Bookwalter, Pat, 166
Boone, Tom, 70
Bradley, Tom, *93*
Brand
  Gustav, 111
  Myles, *150*, 151
Breaking Away, 113
Brier, Amy, 83
Brodeur, Lawrence, 34
Bronxville, 194
Brown
  Barry, 39
  Charlie, 34, 37
  Liz, 73
Brown County, 84, 124, 133
Bryan Park, 85, 127, 155
  Beast, 82
  Pool, 128, 129, 130
  Water slide, 129
Building Association of South Central Indiana, 162
Bus barn, 193
Buskirk, 111

Butler
    Reverend Ernest (Ernie), 32, 40, 135, 199, 201, 209
    Jim, 32
    Park, 135
Bybee Stone, 84, 85, 127

C

CSX (Railroad), 103, 135-136, 149
Caldwell
    and Drake, 110
    Lynton, 56
California, 2, 4, 5, 15, 37, 51, 123
Camiros, 157-159, 161, 163, 176, 177
Cares, 140
Carmony, Paul, 116
Carolers, 209
Cascades
    Golf Course, 131
    Park, 85, 125, 130
Chamber of Commerce, 49, 143, 164, 181, 184, 195
Channel 6 TV, 92
Child Care Food Program, 140
China, 79, 81
Christian Center, 6
Christmas Canopy of Lights, 101
Circuit Court, 42, 120, 133
Citizens for Good Government (CGG), 6, 9, 10, 196
City
    Arts Commission, 83, 85, 127
    Attorney, 24, 32
    Board of Public Safety, 32, 33, 35, 38, 40, 41
    Board of Public Works, 149
    Comptroller, 16, 20, 124, 128, 132, 143, 197, 198, 199, 208

Corporate Counsel, 20, 148, 149
Council, 7, 11, 12, 13, 18, 19, 44, 47, 54, 55, 67, 72, 73, 90,
    91, 92, 94, 99, 123, 126, 127, 130, 144, 147, 148, 149, 150,
    153, 155, 163, 164, 165, 169, 170, 173, 175, 178, 179, 184,
    185, 186, 187, 188, 196, 197, 206, 208
/County Parks District, 123, 124, 129
Court, 108
logo, 67-68
Claremont, 5, 201
Clark
    Ivan, 113
    Petula, 98
Clean Cities, 99, 126
Clear Creek Trail, 135, 136
Clendenning, Gary, 32
Cole, Pat, 153
College Mall, 158, 159, 162, 163, 169, 170, 172, 174, 185, 186,
    189
Columbus (Indiana), 71, 77, 110
Commercial growth, 157, 171, 188
Commission for Bloomington Downtown, 100
Community
    Action Program (CAP), 32, 140
    Development Block Grant, 138
    Development Conference (CDC), 6, 8, 125, 201
    Foundation (Bloomington and Monroe County), 75-78,
        140, 153
    Gardens, 129
    Land Trust, 137
    Radio, 109
Computer technology, 132
Congresses (planning), 160
Connors, Shirley, 8, 9
Consensus, 8, 28, 116, 184, 195, 197-198, 201, 203, 204

Conservancy district, 132-134
Convention Center, 93, 101, 102, 105, 158, 160, 181
Cook
    Bill, 100, 101, 102, 114, 117, 177, 179, 203
    CFC, 71, 78, 100-103, 105, 114, 148, 149, 151, 177, 178
    Condominium, 143, 177, 179
    Enterprises, 143
    Gothic, 178, 180
    Jean, 52
COPA. *See* PCBs
Coppock, Talisha, 100
Core neighborhoods, 88, 160-162, 176. *See also* Neighborhoods
Corso, Lee, 29
Counterfeit journalism, 35
Country Club Road, 135
County. *See* Monroe County
Coverly, Dave, *182*
Coyne, Lynn, 162
Crane Naval Weapons Support Center, 30
Cravens, Oscar H., 111
Crestmont, 6, 126
Crose, Ronald, 87
Crowell, Sears, 9
Cumulative capital fund, 125, 128, 129, 135
Curry
    Building, 117
    Pike, 186

D-E

Davis
    Janine, 115
    Mike, 90, 147, 169
Dawson, Greg, 119

Day Care Resources, 140
Deckard, Joel, 1, 15
DeKoker, Lester, 114, 118, 120-121
Demetrius, Rebecca, 74
Democratic Party, 7, 8, 12, 15, 16, 44, 47, 48, 58, 62, 63, 71, 73, 91, 155, 168, 169, 183, 196
Density, 80, 103, 156, 169, 182
Deputy Mayor, 20, 147, 169
Developers, 91, 92, 122, 124, 155-160, 162, 165, 168, 172-173, 180, 185-186, 190, 204
Dickinson, Emily, 104
Dieter, Mary, 16, 117
Dillon, Robert, 151
Dimetrodon (limestone dinosaur bench), *84*
Dinsmoor
    James (Jim), 6, 196
    Kay, 9, 51, *52*
Dixon
    Polly, 126, 196
    Tom, 126, 196
Downtown, 98-106
    Bloomington, Inc., 101, 102
    owners, 101, 102
Doyle
    Jim, 194
    Charlotte, 197, 199, 201, 204-206, 208, 209
Dunlap, Mary Alice, 50

Eberle, August W., 112, 113
Ehrlich
    Ellen, 86
    Tom, 86
Elkins, Terry, 173

Ellettsville (Indiana), 85, 127, 192
Ellettsville Journal, 113
Elliot Stone Co., 153
Ellis, Tim, 71, 74
Elm Heights, 82, 155, 161
Emergency Shelter Grants, 140
Enchanted Forest, 126
Endwright, Maurice, 113
Engel, Leila, 9
Enochs, F. D. R., 87
Environmental
    Commission, 191-192
    Protection Agency (EPA), 54, 55, 56, 57, 58, 59, 60, 61, 63,
        207, 208
Ernest D. Butler Park. *See* Butler
Eutrophication, 124, 132

F-G

Facilitative leadership, 194-209
Factions (planning), 118, 159
Family airplane, 68, *69*, 70
Faris, Bud, 143
Farmers' Market, 104, 152, 206
Ferguson, Steve, 101, 118, 148, 151
Fernandez, John, 103, 104, 165-169, 183, *209*
Fielder, Jim, 88-89
Finch, Bill, 165, 166, 167, 178, 189
Fire
    Chief, 24, 49
    Fighter, female, 73
    Stations, 20, 107, 108, 142, 148, 183, 208
First National Bank, 100
Fluck Stone, 85

Fountain
    Showers, 153, *154*
    Square Mall, 78, 100, 102, 105
Fourth of July Parade, 100
Frank Southern
    Center, 130, 131
    Ice Arena, 131
Fraser, Rosemary, 85
Fresno, 5, 201
Friedlander, Ken, 191

Gallagher, Tom, 100
Gates Development, 185
Gentry, 111
Geographic Information System (GIS), 90, 192
German band, 96
Ghetto Bloomington, 181
Gilliam, Clarence, 39
Gionet, Dave, 193
Glenn, Patricia, 39
Goldberg, Brad, 153
Goo Goos, 7, 10
Graham Hotel, 98, 100, 102, 203
Grandma Bloomington, 94
Griffy
    Lake, 123, 124, 125, 129, 130, 132
    Nature Preserve, 132, 133
Grodner, Jeff, 90
Gross, Patricia (Pat), 16, 17, 55
Growth Policies Plan, 166, 173, 174, 180, 184, 185

H

Hackett, John, 147
Hailey, Richard, 40, 41, 42
Hall
    Sharon, 79, 80
    Signs, 186, 187
Hamilton, Lee, 73
Hammontree, Bob, 100
Hancock, Dave, 116
Hanna, Bill, 112
Harrison, Mick, 90
Haverstock, James, 32
Hays, Jerry, 138
Helene's House, 140
Hendrix, James, 144
Henegar, Warren, 112, 115
Henke, Tim, 172, 173, 181, 182
Henley Stone Co., 110
Highland Village, 187
Historic districts, 161
Hoadley, 85
Hogan, Steve, 89, 163, 168, 169, 171
Hook-ons, 192
Hoosier
    Hills Food Bank, 140
    House, 140
Hoosierfest, 83
Hopkins
    Anabel, 52
    Jack, 140, 174
Hospital, 106, 177
House, Marilyn, 167, 170
Housing codes, 161

Hot Line (*Herald-Telephone*), 69, 70, 71
Human Resources, 139, 199
Huss, Lee, 99, 127

I-J

Independent
    Limestone, 85
    Voters Party, 89
Indiana Association of Cities and Towns (IACT), 103, 149
Indiana Daily Student (IDS), 34, 48, 114
Indiana Department of Environmental Management (IDEM),
    55, 56, 90
Indiana Limestone Sculpture Symposium, 85
Indiana Policy Review, 180, 181
Indiana Public Interest Research Group (INPIRG), 90
Indiana University
    Afro-American Studies, 32, 39
    Board of Trustees, 148
    Department of
        African American and African Diaspora Studies, 42
        Sociology, 18
    Law School, 32
    School of
        Business, 77
        Medicine, 36, 38
        Music, 26, 89
        Public and Environmental Affairs (SPEA), 132
    Simon Hall, 83
Indianapolis, 27, 37, 38, 40, 70, 92, 149
Infrastructure, 20, 88, 135, 136, 138, 142, 161, 168, 170, 183,
    189, 190, 192, 193, 198

Inn of the Four Winds, 47
Irvine, John, 112
IVY Tech, 109

Jackson Creek
    Trail, 135
    Watershed, 125, 135
Jacobs
    Jane, 6, 99, 201
    Natasha, 88, 161
Jarrels, Edward, 30
Jasper (Indiana), 27
Jeffries, Patricia, 169
Johnson
    Dairy Products (building), 147
    President Lyndon, 8, 196
Jones
    Bill, 132
    Doug, 180, 181
    Reverend Marvin, 6, 125
Jordan River, 192
Justice Building, 104, 107, 109, 120-121

K-L

Karaganis, Joseph, 55, 56
Karst
    Farm Park, 129, 130
    topography, 58
Keller, Randall, 30, 31, 41
Kentucky Colonels, 95
King
    Douglas, 41
    Martin Luther, 8, 40

Kid City, 136, 183, 202
Kiesling, Iris, 165, 166, 168, 179
Kirkwood Street, 85, 98, 99, 185
Kiwanis, 91
Knight, Bobby, 79
Kramer, Carolyn, 112
Kruzan, Mark, 104, 183

Ladwig, T. Craig, 180, 181
Lake Lemon, 123-126, 130-132
    Conservancy District, 132
Langley, John, 33, 48, 72, 89
Latimer Woods (pocket park), 135
League of Women Voters, 90, 196
Leaves (disposal), 191
Lemon
    Lane, 54, 56
    Tom, 50
Leonard Springs, 123, 130
Liesmann, Ronald, 32, 38
Lilly Foundation, 78
Limestone
    bench carving contest, 83, 85, 127
    Institute, 83
Lipkin, Harriet, 128
Livable cities, 104
Louisville Courier-Journal, 16
Los Angeles, 5, 15, 37, 93, 201
Lotus Music Festival, 104
Loyalty oath (California), 4
Luchow (Taiwan), 79-81
Lunch Bunch, 51-52

M

Madera (California), 2, 3, 201
Mahurin, Marshall, 110
Main Street Program, 99
Maine, 85, 86
Mall sprawl, 167
Mandel, Mark, 114
Martin
    Richard, 55, 161
    Sue, 9, 10, *46*
Master Plan, 20, 90, 92, 125, 131, 135, 156-160, 162-174, 177,
        178, 180, 181, 182, 184, 187, 204, 205
    codes, 166
Matchstick Program, 76, 78
Matheu, Christine, 149
Matthews, 111
Mayer, Tim, 67
McCarthy
    Eugene, 6, 196
    Joe, 86
McCloskey, Frank, 1, 7, 12, 16, 17, 47, 54, 55, 58, 73, 98, 102,
    127, 143, *152*, 167, 191, 203, 207
McCluskey, John, 32
Mental Health Center, 140
Merrifield, Norm, 128, 202
Merriman, Betty, 128
Michigan
    Ann Arbor, 5, 123, 194, 201
    University of, 6
Middle Way House, 140

Miller
    Henry, 30
    J. Irwin, 77
    Rosemary, 107-109, 121, 122
Mills Pool, 131
Minneapolis (Minnesota), 103, 149, 173
Missionaries, 80
Moir, Denny, 100, 101
Mom, 25
Monroe County
    Coroner, 33, 35, 36
    Courthouse, 96, 109-122, 204
    Housing Solutions, 139, 177
    Option Income Tax, 129, 130, 148
    Public Library, 21, 105, 106, 110, 155, 160, 184, 202
Monroe Water Treatment Plant, 192
Monsanto, 53
Moores Pike, 172
Morgan, Kevin, 115
Morris, Tim, 29-30
Morrison
    Glenda, 99, 101. *See also* Murray, Glenda
    Jack, 44, 49, 50, 51, 71
Morrow, Bill, 143
Morton Street, 144
Mueller, Tim, 158-162, 171, 174, 176, 178, 180, 181
Mulholland, Jack, 77
Municipal Building, 16, 47, 163, 164, 184. *See also* City Hall
Murphy, Jim, *150*, 151
Murray, Glenda, 197. *See also* Morrison, Glenda
Music in the Parks, 126
Mutz, John (Lieutenant Governor), 71
Mysterious Stranger, 50

N-O

Najam, Ted, 165, 167
National
    Association for the Advancement of Colored People
        (NAACP), 39
    Organization of Women (NOW), 47, 51
    Register of Historic Places, 115
Natural
    Resources Commission, 133, 134
    Resources, Department of, 134
Neale, Charles, 159, 163
Neal's Landfill, 54
Neighborhoods, 20, 88, 90, 99, 103, 155-162, 172, 173, 176, 201,
    204. *See also* Core neighborhoods
Newman, Paul, 79, 81
Nick's English Hut, 18
Ninth Street Park, 125, 130, 135
No-growth policy, 163, 166
Nurre Company, 144

O'Brien, Tom, 16, 17
Occidental College, 5, 18
O'Connor incinerator, 60
Odle, McGuire and Shook, 149
Odle-Burke Architects, 116, 119
Olcott
    Lloyd, 102, 126, 135, *150,* 151, 166, 168
    Park, 135
Older Americans Center, 91, 129
Open
    door policy, 200
    Space Acquisition Fund, 125, 135
Opportunity House, 23, 24

Orr, Governor Robert D., 71
Out lot, 164-167
Outdoor stage, 126, 152
Owen, Kent, 44

P

Paoli (Indiana), 166
Park(s)
    and Recreation, 83, 100, 105, 123-136, 143, 166
    Board, 124, 206
    Department, 124, 126, 127, 129, 132, 135, 202
    Foundation Fund, 135
Parking, 88, 96, 98, 100-102, 105, 121, 122, 129, 142, 147, 150,
       151, 152, 156, 162, 166, 171, 175, 177, 179
    Garage, 98, 102, 147-148, 183, 203
    Permits, 162, 175
Parkwood East (pocket park), 135
Parr, Virginia, 114
Patterson
    Pat, 21, 128, 190, 191
    Pat's jar, 21
PCBs, 53-61, 63, 87, 92, 184, 206, 208
    Allison in Wonderland, 63
    Bacteria, 63
    Cleanup, 49, 54-61, 63, 72, 73, 89, 90, 207
        cost, 56
        incineration, 55, 57, 58, 59, 63, 89-92, 207
        local control, 55, 56, 63, 72, 207
        megalith, 59
        method, 57, 58, 59, 207
        permit standard, 57, 60
        publicity, 58
        sunlight, 63

Consent Decree, 55-63, 72, 89, 92, 207
COPA (The Coalition Opposed to PCB Ash in Monroe
    County, Inc.), 58, 89
Sludge, 54
Toxicity, 53, 59
Peace groups, 196
Peckham, Guyton and Viets, 101
Penney, J. C., 114
People Against the Incinerator (PATI), 88
People's Park, 85, 127
Peoples, Rick, 54
Phillips
    Harvey, 91, 100, 126
    Mike, 128, 133, 136, 192
Pierce, Matt, 90, 92
Pless, John, 36, 37, 38
Poplars, 92
Positive Progress, Inc., 180
Post Office, 106
Prall, Fred, 100
Predatory investors, 161-62
Preus, Betty Rae, 47, 51, *52*
Princess (Theater), 23, 24, 25, 101
Priorities, 20, 142, 190, 198
Pro-plan policy, 166
Prospect Hill, 161
Public forums (planning), 159, 173
Public Health Nursing, 140
Public Transit. *See* Bloomington Public Transit
Puck Players, 125

Q-R

Quality Growth, Inc., 161
Quebec City, 86
Queen Tomi, 64

RCA, 138, 145, 146
ROTC (Reserve Officers Training Corps), 97
Radio stations
    WFHB (community), 109
    WFIU (Indiana University), 94
Ragan, Frank, 124, 127, 128, 130
Rails-to-Trails, 103, 104, 135, 136
Ralph Mills (Pool), 130
Ralston
    Bob, 78
    Ilknur, 78
Rape Crisis Center. *See* Middle Way House
Ratcliff, Jimmy, 30, 31, 41
Rechter, Richard, 163, 169-172
Recycling, 95, 99, 183, 191, 192
    bins, 95
REDACTED, Mr., 44, 45
Redevelopment, 49, 71, 99-102, 104-106, 136-138, 141, 161,
    166, 197, 203, 204
Regester
    Center Parking Garage, 147
    Jim, 163, 168
Renneisen, Mick, 134, *209*
Research park, 93, 147-149, 205
Residential growth, 157, 162
Reinhard, Bill, 120
Remonstrance, 112, 115, 117, 119, 120, 128, 131
Revitalization, 20, 88, 99, 100, 104, 126, 143, 146, 147, 183

Rhinehart, Ted, 128
Richardson, Jeff, 7, 12, 196
Riddle Point, 130, 131
Riley, Phil, 32, 33, 36
Roberts, Clarence, 36
Rodgers, David, 85
Rogers Farm, 169
Rogers/Rockport Road, 157
Rooster, 22-23
Rotary Club, 59, 91, 92
Roush, Rosalie, 161
Ruckman, Chuck, 128, 143, 146, 147
Ruh, Henry, 113
Runkle, Linda, 128, 148, 149
Russell, Joseph, 39
Ryan, John, 42

S

St. Croix, Brian de, 11
Sam's Club, 171, 174
Sanitation, 191
San Joaquin Valley, 2, 4, 201
Sarah Lawrence College, 194
Sare Road, 172
Save
    Our Taxes Committee, 112-115, 117, 118, 120
    the Courthouse Rally, 118
Schmaltz, Dick, *44*, 98, 100
Schrader, Bill, 100
Self sufficiency, 140, 141, 202
Senior Citizens, 87, 136
    Drug Prescription Project, 140

Nutrition Project, 140

Service, Pam, 126, 153, 165, 187

Sewer, 20, 54, 58, 111, 138, 191, 192

Sharp, Steve, 30

Sherman, Jim, 180

Sherwood Oaks II (park), 135

Shields, Brooke, 71

Shopping centers, 158, 161, 164, 165, 166, 177, 185, 204

Showers, 111

    City Hall, 88, 93, 103, 104, 142, 150, 151, 154, 173, 183, 205, 206

    Furniture Company, 104, 143-149, 205

Simon Hall. *See* Indiana University

Sister City Program, 79

Skowhegan (Maine), 86

Slogan, 63, 99

Smiley, Tavis, 32, 33

Smith

    Ambrosia, 29, 42, 43

    Cynequa, 29, 32, 40, 41, 42

    Denver, 29-43

    John, 183

    Margaret Chase, 85-86

    Ron, 89, 90, 91, 169

    Steve, 181

    William, 39

Snake Alley (Taipei), 80

Snoddy, Bob, 100

Southern

    Christian Leadership Conference, 39

    Mayors Round Table, 27

    Sporting Goods, 6

Southwest Quadrant, 125, 135, 192

Spanker's Branch, 192

Spiek, Chris, 137, 138, 141
Stafford, Bea, 52
State
    Board of Tax Commissioners, 120
    of the City address, 45, 60, 77, 184
Stein, Devonia, 52
Steroids, 37, 38
Stewart, Bob, 71
Stolberg, Eric, 162
Stover, Rebecca, 83
Street flooding, 191
Streeter, Willie, 129
Strip mall, 169, 171, 185, 186
Student housing, 103, 155, 156
Sturbaum, Chris, 161
Suburban subdivisions, 156
Sun Moon Lake (Taiwan), 80
Superfund law, 56, 207
Survey (planning), 157, 158
Swafford, Tom, 163, 168, 178

T

Taipei, 80
Taiwan, 79, 80, 81
Tapp Road, 157
Taste of Bloomington, 102
Tax
    Abatement, 103, 105, 179, 203
    County Income, 129, 130
    Freeze, 190
    Increment Finance (TIF), 103, 105
Taylorcraft, 68
Taylor, William, 37
Television (local access), 21, 55, 94, 165, 179

Third Street City Hall, 142-143. *See also* City Hall
Third Street Park, 91, 105, 130
Thomson
    Community Park, 135
    Inc., 136
    /RCA, 138
Tinder, John, 41
Tischler, Alice, 52
Tolen, Jim, 187
Tom O'Daniel Ford, 102
Tourist and Convention Center, 160
Towell, Al, 9, 16, 17, 18, 44, 71-73
Tox-Away Day, 192
Traffic Congestion, 156, 163, 174
Transit Board, 193. *See also* Bloomington Public Transit
Tree City, 99, 126, 127
Trinkle, Phyllis, 32
Tuba Santas, 100, 126
Tucson (Arizona), 63, 90
Twin Lakes, 123, 124, 130, 134
    Sports Park, 134

U, V, W

Unions, 8, 91, 145
Upland (California), 5, 201
Upper Cascades Park, 130
Urban, 149, 177, 192
    Forest Plan, 125
    Sprawl, 157, 181
User fees, 123, 131
Utilities, 20, 56, 58, 72, 87, 89, 90, 123-125, 128, 129, 132-136, 179, 191, 192, 199, 207

Van der Dussen, Kurt, 115, 119, 121
Vazsonyi, Belint, 89-93, 168
Veto, 166, 167, 168, 170, 207
Vice President (class), 7, 65
Vietnam, 6, 8, 30, 195
Volunteer Action Network, 140
Volunteers, 9, 18, 48, 78, 109, 127, 139, 184, 195
Voters' Union, 8, 9

Wagner, Don, 44, 116
Waicukauski, Ron, 39
Wal-Mart, 171, 174
Waldron, 111
    Arts Center, 101, 107, 109, 122
    Cecile, 108
    John, 107, 109
Wampler, Basil
Wapahani, 130
Water, 20, 72, 89, 123, 130, 132, 133, 138, 177, 185, 190-192, 206
Water slide. *See* Bryan Park
Watson, James E., 111
Weathervane, 103, 110
Weddings, 65-67
Weddle, Harold, 24
Weekly Courier, 111
Wells, Herman B, *76*, 77, 85, 108, *151*
West Baden Hotel, 110
West Side, 48, 49, 75, 125, 126, 162, 163, 171, 173, 176, 185-189,
    201, 202, 205, 206
    Community Center, 130
    industries, 191
Westinghouse, 53-58, 60, 72, 73, 207
Wheeler, Sue, 78, 139, 140, 141
White, Kirk, 167, 171, 183

Whitehall Crossing, 185, 187, 188
Wicks Department Store, 100
Wiggins, Bill, 42
Wilhelm, E. A., 149
Williams, Patricia, 16, 51, *52*
Wininger-Stolberg Group, 164, 172
Winslow Sports Complex, 129
Wissing, Kathleen, 78
Women (status), 47, 72, 87, 145
Women's International League for Peace and Freedom
    (WILPF), 196
Wood, John, 178
Woolery Mill, 85
Workforce Development Program, 140
Workingmen's Federal Savings and Loan, 138

Y-Z

Yankee Stadium, 82
Yates, Peter, 113
Young, Rod, 170, 180
Zebendon, Chuck, 100
Zietlow, Charlotte, 9, 16, 58, 62, 116, 117, 118, 121
Zoning, 100, 155-189, 203, 204
    densities, 101, 103, 155-156, 176
    ordinances, 101, 103, 105, 166, 173, 175, 177, 180, 181, 182,
        184, 185, 186, 205
    policy, 159, 177, 201
    regulations, 164, 204
    variances, 177

VITAE

TOMILEA JOYCE ALLISON *(nee Radosevich)*

Born Madera, California, 3/28/34
Graduate, Madera High School, 1951
A.B., Occidental College, 1955
Deputy Probation Officer, Fresno County, California, 1956-58
Deputy Probation Officer, San Bernardino County, 1958-59
Married James Allison, 1958
Daughter Devon, born 1959
Daughter Leigh, born 1961

Bloomington City Council: At Large Member, 1977-83
Mayor, City of Bloomington, 1983-95

HONORS:
Russell G. Lloyd Distinguished Service Award, Indiana Association of
    Cities and Towns
Special Recognition, U.S. Conference of Mayors, 1993
Sagamore of the Wabash (Governor Bayh)
Kentucky Colonel (Governor Martha Layne Collins)
Monroe County Hall of Fame, 2007
Lifetime Achievement Award, Women's History Month, 2010
President, Indiana Association of Cities and Towns, 1993-94
Mayor of the Year, Murat Temple, 1995
Citizen of the Year, National Association of Social Workers, 1991
Lifetime Achievement Award, Greater Bloomington Chamber of
    Commerce, 1995

OTHER:
Co-founder, Community Development Conference, Bloomington
Co-founder, Citizens for Good Government, Monroe County
Co-founder, Bloomington Branch, Women's International League for
    Peace and Freedom
Founder, Commission for Bloomington Downtown
Co-founder, Verify the Vote, Monroe County
Co-founder, Move to Amend-South Central Indiana, 2012
Instigated the founding of the Community Foundation of Bloomington and
    Monroe County

JAMES ALLISON

Born Porterville, California, December 23, 1932
Graduate, Roosevelt High School, Fresno, 1950
A.B., University of California at Berkeley, 1954
U.S. Army, 1954-56
Deputy Probation Officer, Fresno County, California, 1957
M.A., Claremont Graduate School, 1960
Ph.D., University of Michigan, 1963
Assistant Professor-Professor, Department of Psychology,
    Indiana University-Bloomington, 1963-1992

HONORS:

Creative Talent Award, American Institutes for Research, 1964
Sigma Xi
Distinguished Teaching Award, Indiana University Class of 1968

CPSIA information can be obtained at www.ICGtesting.com
Printed in the USA
BVOW06s1741290715

411000BV00012B/92/P

9 781514 253144